Oral and Nonverbal Expression

Ivan Muse

Routledge
Taylor & Francis Group
New York London

First published 1996 by Eye On Education

Published 2013 by Routledge
711 Third Avenue, New York, NY, 10017, USA
2 Park Square, Milton Park, Abingdon, Oxon OX14 4RN

Routledge is an imprint of the Taylor & Francis Group, an informa business

Library of Congress Cataloging-in-Publication Data

Muse, Ivan,
Oral and nonverbal expression / Ivan Muse
p. cm.
Includes bibliographical references.
ISBN 1-883001-27-7
1. Oral communication. 2. Communication in education.
I. Title.
P95.M86 1886 96-20366
302.2'264—dc20 CIP

ISBN: 978-1-883001-27-8 (pbk)

Published by Eye On Education:

Block Scheduling: A Catalyst for Change in High Schools
by Robert Lynn Canady and Michael D. Rettig

Teaching in the Block: Strategies for Engaging Active Learners
edited by Robert Lynn Canady and Michael D. Rettig

Educational Technology: Best Practices from America's Schools
by William C. Bozeman and Donna J. Baumbach

The Educator's Brief Guide to Computers in the Schools
by Eugene F. Provenzo, Jr.

Handbook of Educational Terms and Applications
by Arthur K. Ellis and Jeffrey T. Fouts

Research on Educational Innovations
by Arthur K. Ellis and Jeffrey T. Fouts

Research on School Restructuring
by Arthur K. Ellis and Jeffrey T. Fouts

Hands-on Leadership Tools for Principals
by Ray Calabrese, Gary Short, and Sally Zepeda

The Principal's Edge
by Jack McCall

The Administrator's Guide to School-Community Relations
by George E. Pawlas

Leadership: A Relevant and Realistic Role for Principals
by Gary M. Crow, L. Joseph Matthews, and Lloyd E. McCleary

Organizational Oversight:
Planning and Scheduling for Effectiveness
by David A. Erlandson, Peggy L. Stark, and Sharon M. Ward

Motivating Others: Creating the Conditions
by David P. Thompson

The School Portfolio:
A Comprehensive Framework for School Improvement
by Victoria L. Bernhardt

School-to-Work
by Arnold H. Packer and Marion W. Pines

Innovations in Parent and Family Involvement
by William Rioux and Nancy Berla

The Performance Assessment Handbook
Volume 1: Portfolios and Socratic Seminars
by Bil Johnson

The Performance Assessment Handbook
Volume 2: Performances and Exhibitions
by Bil Johnson

Bringing the NCTM Standards to Life
by Lisa B. Owen and Charles E. Lamb

Mathematics the Write Way
by Marilyn S. Neil

Transforming Education Through Total Quality Management: A Practitioner's Guide
by Franklin P. Schargel

Quality and Education: Critical Linkages
by Betty L. McCormick

The Educator's Guide to Implementing Outcomes
by William J. Smith

Schools for All Learners: Beyond the Bell Curve
by Renfro C. Manning

Foreword

The School Leadership Library was designed to show practicing and aspiring principals what they should know and be able to do to be effective leaders of their schools. The books in this series were written to answer the question, "How can we improve our schools by improving the effectiveness of our principals?"

Success in the principalship, like in other professions, requires mastery of a knowledge and skills base. One of the goals of the National Policy Board for Educational Administration (sponsored by NAESP, NASSP, AASA, ASCD, NCPEA, UCEA, and other professional organizations) was to define and organize that knowledge and skill base. The result of our efforts was the development of a set of 21 "domains," building blocks representing the core understandings and capabilities required of successful principals.

The 21 domains of knowledge and skills are organized under four broad areas: Functional, Programmatic, Interpersonal and Contextual. They are as follows:

FUNCTIONAL DOMAINS
- Leadership
- Information Collection
- Problem Analysis
- Judgment
- Organizational Oversight
- Implementation
- Delegation

PROGRAMMATIC DOMAINS
- Instruction and the Learning Environment
- Curriculum Design
- Student Guidance and Development
- Staff Development
- Measurement and Evaluation
- Resource Allocation

INTERPERSONAL DOMAINS
- Motivating Others
- Interpersonal Sensitivity
- Oral and Nonverbal Expression
- Written Expression

CONTEXTUAL DOMAINS
- Philosophical and Cultural Values
- Legal and Regulatory Applications
- Policy and Political Influences
- Public Relations

These domains are not discrete, separate entities. Rather, they evolved only for the purpose of providing manageable descriptions of essential content and practice so as to better understand the entire complex role of the principalship. Because human behavior comes in "bunches" rather than neat packages, they are also overlapping pieces of a complex puzzle. Consider the domains as converging streams of behavior that spill over one another's banks but that all contribute to the total reservoir of knowledge and skills required of today's principals.

The School Leadership Library was established by General Editors David Erlandson and Al Wilson to provide a broad examination of the content and skills in all of the domains. The authors of each volume in this series offer concrete and realistic illustrations and examples, along with reflective exercises. You will find their work to be of exceptional merit, illustrating with insight the depth and interconnectedness of the domains. This series provides the fullest, most contemporary, and most useful information available for the preparation and professional development of principals.

Scott D. Thomson
Executive Secretary
National Policy Board for
Educational Administration

About the Author

Ivan D. Muse is a Professor in the Department of Educational Leadership at Brigham Young University. After teaching high school science in Tucson, Arizona, he attended Stanford University as a doctoral student and then served as a high school administrator in Santa Maria, California for four years. Offered a teaching assistantship at the University of Utah, he completed the Ed.D. in 1967. He served as a high school principal at The Cherry Creek School District in Denver, Colorado before assuming a professorship at Brigham Young University.

During the past two decades in higher education, Dr. Muse has authored numerous articles, book chapters and monographs on topics ranging from rural education to school leadership. He has served as Chair of the Department of Educational Leadership since 1991. Within the past 10 years, his department has received the LEAD grant for administrator preparation, three Danforth Foundation grants and a grant from the Utah State Board of Education for the preparation of school leaders. The Leaders Preparation Program (LPP) is nationally recognized as one of the best administrator preparation programs in the country. BYU and three other prominent universities have been funded since 1992 to form an Alliance for the Improvement of School Leadership. In addition, he developed the statewide Mentor Principal Preparation Program and has recently initiated the School District Teacher Leader M.ED. Program.

PREFACE

Leaders of quality are explosively demanding exceptional resources as they continue their quest to do better. Such resources must assist the leader in developing sensible reasoning and quality practice for both the present and future.

Oral and nonverbal expression has been written to assist leaders as they apply one of the twenty-one domains identified by the National Policy Board for Educational Administration. This book comprehensively addresses salient information regarding verbal and nonverbal interaction. Ivan Muse has written specifically about the process of communication which encompasses the active process of oral interaction, the use and understanding of nonverbal behavior, the essence of listening, being sensitive in word and comments, communicating within groups and interacting with difficult people. The final chapter guides the leader in preparing and delivering a quality speech. Practical applications for successful communication are provided to assist the reader in becoming ever more accomplished through enhancing both verbal and nonverbal proficiency. Oral and nonverbal skills are unceasingly practiced throughout a school leader's day. Without question, such skills are those continually put to use by principals who overcome barriers, gain support, and assist others in enhancing the learning of our youth.

Those who practice leadership in school settings are expected to do well. The demand has quickened for exceptionally skilled school leaders who continually hone their abilities in a never-ending quest to be better today than yesterday and better tomorrow than today. Such leaders must practice quality oral and nonverbal expression.

The twenty-first century is now. Younger children enrolled in today's schools will graduate when more than a tenth of the next century has passed. They need school leaders who practice twenty-first century communication skills. This book is a valued resource in providing up-to-date strategies, skills, and user friendly resources for school leaders.

David A. Erlandson
Alfred P. Wilson

TABLE OF CONTENTS

INTRODUCTION

Individuals in school leadership positions face a variety of tasks and challenges in running a successful school program. One of the most difficult challenges faced by the administrator involves dealing with people. Daily the school leader interacts with teachers, students and staff, encouraging group goals, good teaching and motivated learning. Good communication is also necessary to convey to parents, community and school superiors the vision of the school and the realities of school operations and relationships.

Two observations can be made about effective school principals. First, they are noted by a diversity of leadership styles. In some cases, effective principals are energetic, aggressive and seemingly involved in everything happening in the school. In other cases, the principals are quiet, nurturing and supportive, often delegating tasks to others. Regardless of their leadership style, effective principals all seem to focus on active leadership. This involves motivating students, encouraging staff to better performance, reaching out to the community and continually improving the school environment. These principals rely on communication and a visible presence with individuals and groups in the school as well as parents in the community and in building positive school images.

School administrators constantly use oral communication to articulate a vision of the school, to motivate others, to defend decisions, to persuade, to explain school changes and innovations and to listen to others. Because the principal is the one person who is directly involved in every aspect of the school's operation, consistent, clear and meaningful communication is an important function. The principal has a responsibility to keep everyone involved with the school informed about what is happening at the school and what progress is being made to meet educational goals.

Principals are expected to be good communicators, but formal training in communication techniques at the college level is often lacking. When it does occur, the emphasis tends to focus upon techniques in writing and composing effective newsletters or giving speeches to large groups. Ways to improve oral communication and listen more effectively receive insufficient attention.

In this book, an attempt is made to cover, in a comprehensive manner, the most important aspects of oral communication. Each chapter offers practical applications in interacting successfully with others in a number of situations. Since much of a principal's interaction with others is oral or spoken, rather than written and face-to-face rather than by telephone or memo, each communication act will largely determine the type of relationship that principals will have with others. Regardless of how well you think that you communicate, it is always helpful to pause and rethink your oral communication skills. As you read this book, you will find that many of the ideas are common sense while some will be new. Hopefully, your reading will help you to become a better speaker and listener and more effective as a school leader.

1

When the Principal Speaks—Everyone Listens

Communication is a process of sharing experience till it becomes a common possession. It modifies the disposition of both parties who partake of it. —John Dewey

The social lives and the work of humans involves a constant interplay of communication with individuals and groups. Most school administrators are aware that of all the knowledge and skills that they possess, that of creating information and communicating with others ranks at the top in terms of importance. Principals are involved constantly with communication in all that they say and do. Through interpersonal relationships, principals interact with teachers, students, staff and parents on a daily basis. The effect of this interaction establishes relationships and professional harmony with associates. Through group communication, principals interact with others, sharing experiences and ideas, solving problems, handling conflicts, articulating beliefs and values, and building trust and rapport.

On occasion, even the best of communication intent by the principal can diminish relationships and cause interpersonal conflict and anxiety. Not surprisingly, there may be in some schools as much poor communication as there is good. Some type of consequence to communication will always occur because individuals on the receiving end of the process interpret messages with differing meaning. Often, the meaning of a message is considered on a continuum of rightness or wrongness. The degree of personal acceptance of a message may relate to its timing, the receivers field of experience with the sender, message interpretation, personal involvement, etc.

Communication is the glue that binds every school organization together. Developing, giving and sharing information links individuals and groups together in the common task of effectively operating the school program. The school administrator is responsible for setting school objectives, organizing tasks, motivating teachers and students, informing parents, evaluating school program results and making decisions. In this key position, it is obvious that when the principal speaks, everyone listens. Without a clear understanding of the process of communication and the ability and desire to communicate effectively, the work of the principal will be diminished and the school will not run well.

The communication process involves the exchange of information in some manner between a sender and a receiver. In most instances, whether well planned or hurriedly delivered, the sender hopes that the message will be received exactly as it was intended. Unfortunately, barriers to successful communication frequently occur and cause the transmission and the message itself, to be distorted.

Exchanging information in the school is an ongoing process and seems simple, and at other times complex. On occasion, it is necessary to convey information rapidly without considering how the information will be received. Often, principals must react to emergencies and rely on judgment and common sense to resolve problems and handle conflicts. I can recall one of those critical moments when the importance of communication lay heavily on my mind.

The day, the place and the time are etched in my memory just as vividly as words chiseled out of granite on a memorial in a park. What would I say to 1300 high school students, 46 teachers and 12 office workers? The P.A. system was on, my voice would soon reach all of those in the school building, yet I was hesitant. My own emotions were running like a river cascading out of control over high falls and cracking on the rocks below.

My secretary was standing by her desk, her fists clenched, cheeks drawn and tears welling in her eyes. There was no question whether or not this message would be misunderstood. The concern was, could I deliver the message in a calm and controlled manner and expect the listeners to likewise manage the information without becoming completely "unglued" or emotionally distraught.

I clutched the grey metallic microphone in my hand and clicked the "on" button with my thumb. I glanced quickly at the clock from habit, straightened my tie and began with a voice surprisingly controlled.

"Dear students, faculty and staff, I am sorry to disturb your classes and school activities at this time, but I do need your complete attention for the following message. I am very sad to report that we have just received news that President John F. Kennedy has been assassinated by a gunman in Dallas, Texas. This comes as a shock to all of us and we will mourn his death. Please remain in your classrooms, and I will keep you informed of the details as they come to us. I also expect that shortly we will receive word from the school superintendent regarding any changes in the school schedule the rest of this day and in the days to come."

I paused, clicked the microphone button to "off" and softly replaced it on the counter. Turning to my secretary, I nodded, "Let's get a memo out to every teacher with instructions on how to handle student concerns, use of radios to listen to the news reports in class, and other problems. Also, call in the counselors and staff members so we can plan supervision between periods and during the lunch hour."

Thankfully, not all communication efforts are as intense and totally involving as the one mentioned. However, most of us have had those times when communication was serious and the situation was "real" and emotionally involved. While I, as many of you, can remember vividly what they were doing on the day President Kennedy was shot, many younger individuals do not feel the impact of that tragic and emotional ordeal. It is difficult to imagine that some 50% or more of our population are now too young to remember the death of President Kennedy. Times and people change and information causes different reactions in different people. The purpose of presenting this scenario is to stress the fact that as school leaders we are emotionally engaged in relationships that require the creation of information and its transmissions. We live in a dynamic society, and communication is a necessary ongoing process that keeps organizations and individuals stable, rational and in harmony with objectives and goals.

Each of us, whether in a school, district office, university, state office of education, etc., lives and works for a large part of our daylight hours within an organizational structure. The organization called education is unique in that the product happens to be students, and the process involves teachers and other educators working to provide information and ideas to young people that will ultimately help them to be successful in life and contribute to a better society.

THE WORK OF THE PRINCIPAL

School administrators are primarily responsible for administering all aspects of the school. The principal in today's school organization has a complex job, requiring a wide range of leadership, supervisory and administrative proficiencies. Because students, teachers, parents and the community play vital roles in shaping the school's mission, responsibilities and character, communication skills are vital to the principal's well-being as a school leader. Few organization executive officers in any work endeavor spend more time at communication, and interact as much with others as the school administrator. It has been reported, and from experience I can testify to its truth, that principals spend 90% of their time interacting with people and 10% of their time interacting with things. Just as a check, when was the last time you were able to spend more than a 10 minute session in a quiet setting with your office computer? Principals often express frustration that they have new computers on their desks and never seem to have time (unless in the evenings) to use them. The situation probably won't change in the foreseeable future.

As school leaders are aware, they typically work some 50 plus hours a week, and much of this time is talking and listening time. Martin and Willower (1981) and Doud (1982) categorized the work of principals into a number of specific tasks. The principals in the study were involved with unscheduled meetings for 27.5% of their time and scheduled meetings for 17.3% of their time. Personal exchanges and conversations involved 14.1% of the principal's involvement, with phone calls taking 5.8% of the time, and classroom and hallway monitoring taking 7.7% of the time. Lastly, the principals had 16% of the day for desk work, which often involved preparing reports, projects and letters that had to be completed by a prescribed deadline. The critical aspect of this data is that face-to-face contact in single individual or group settings involves some 59% of the principal's time on the job. Without question, of the various proficiencies or skills that distinguish outstanding school principals, one of the most important is the ability to communicate effectively.

The better the principal is at communication, the better the school will run. In good schools, school administrators are seen constantly interacting with others in a variety of settings. Proficient principals capitalize on such encounters to honestly and openly address questions and problems, to underscore the school's program and mission and to communicate a positive image of the school.

Realizing that communication is so important, why do there appear to be so many examples of poor communication taking place within the schools? Ask a school superintendent why a particular principal may be having a run on difficult problems, and the answer most often will focus upon communication breakdown. Obviously, communication is more than just a message or a response, and in a large organizational setting, communicating to everyone is no easy task, but the administrator usually receives the blame if a lack of communication is cited as the major cause of a school problem.

Actually, the typical principal is very good at handling the "things" of communication. It is not so difficult to send a message from one location to another, to talk to a student, teacher or parent about a problem involving a school policy, to conduct a structured meeting following an agenda, or even to give a prepared speech to a group of parents or community folks. The difficulty is that, while we expect to control and handle easily the content of our messages as well as the vehicle for communication (memo, newsletter, telephone call, face-to-face interaction, etc.), our listeners perceive these messages in an entirely different personal environment and context. Principals are often too busy, are not aware of, or ignore the signals that indicate communication has gone awry.

Margaret Wheatley (1992) indicates that "information is unique as a resource because of its capacity to generate itself." She concludes, "As long as there are senders and receivers linked together in a context, fertility abounds." Of course, that is a fear that school leaders share. Information can easily be misinterpreted, twisted, enhanced, expanded and so forth, until it becomes totally different from what was originally intended. This is the real context that defines meaningful communication. Information is not just a message plying itself along some physical pathway to be absorbed as purely black or white without any variation of meaning or intent. To think of communication as only a system is to miss the human element that exists within the sender and the receiver. If the principal doesn't communicate well, those with whom he or she works will make up missing dialogue and create their own responses and feelings about the school leader. The organization grapevine, with its vast supply of rumors, thrives on communication that is missing, inadequate or not trusted. Contrary to what may be thought about the old proverb "out of sight, out of mind," that does not hold true for most individuals in any organization. Remember the faculty room when you were a teacher? Miss a noonday session of the members of the "let's roast so and so today" group and you were soon to be the topic of discussion. People like to talk, and they like to generate and nourish information, be it positive or negative, scant or plentiful.

The generation of rumors and inaccurate information about events and individuals is a common characteristic of humans and can't be stopped. As Lemmick (1995) notes, "The brain in individuals craves information, and when it can't come by the data honestly, it does the best it can." Administrators need to recognize the importance of oral communication, the manner in which it is absorbed and used by others, and the value of receiving feedback continually in order to monitor organizational well-being and health.

Responsiveness Communication

Think about your school setting and your relationships with other members in your organization. How responsive have you been to the information that exists in the school, that speaks to your effectiveness? Do you know when you haven't communicated well and when you may have created some conflict or problem that needs to be mended or smoothed over?

Every school employee or student carries within his or her mind an image of the principal. This image is taken into account when the principal produces a message, and this attitude colors the message. Consider, for instance, the following statements from teachers who work for and with a number of differing principals. If the perceptions that they have for their principals are reflected by these comments, how well will any future communications be received? As you read these statements, consider what the principals might have to do to begin to change these perceptions.

- My principal must be under a lot of pressure. She never smiles.
- My principal's favorite statement is, "I'll try to get to it," and he never does.
- My principal always thinks that his ideas are the best.
- I can hardly get a word in edgewise with my principal. He talks just to hear himself speak.
- My principal likes some teachers better than others. He plays favorites.
- Don't bring your problems to my principal, or you will be on her "hit list" of undesirable teachers.
- If you ask my principal to discipline an unruly student, he says, "What do you want me to be—the bad guy?"
- I can't remember the last time that my principal told me that I was doing a good job.

- My principal doesn't act like she thinks what I am saying is very important.
- My principal is nice but not really caring.

The comments made by the teachers above relate specifically to the interaction style of school principals. It is certainly not possible to be everything to everyone, but teachers, as well as others in the workplace, like to feel appreciated and to be accepted as valuable members of the organization. Most of us need to learn more about being sensitive to others. "What is needed," asserts David Bohn (1980), "is an act of understanding in which we see the totality of an actual process." This is an intriguing thought for the work of the principal. Imagine yourself flowing through the school as a wave, lapping upon the beach, touching everything and creating new patterns and structures on the sand. Waves move about everything within their reach and leave some impact on each object, be it the sand, a small tidal pool, or an outcropping of rocks. This natural process sparks within most of us a feeling of peace and relaxation, and even contentment. We feel a part of the setting. Many individuals journey miles for the opportunity to simply sit on a beach and sense the miraculous feeling of being one with nature.

If we shift our attention away from the beach and to the school, the setting changes, but the interpretation can remain the same. It is not difficult to imagine the school principal spending the time to connect with every teacher (workable and difficult), in an attempt to come together, to understand, to communicate, to learn and to grow in harmony. It takes effort to produce harmony and to smooth over feelings of conflict, fear or jealousy. With those that we don't particularly care for (and there are a few around), interweaving a productive relationship can be very challenging. But that is the implied function of the principal: to be a support to others, to seek for harmony and a source of common purpose.

ESTABLISHING POSITIVE RELATIONSHIPS

Positive relationships in the school setting come about primarily through constant interaction with groups and individuals in a variety of settings. These settings range from the familiar (the principal's office, hallway and classroom) to the slightly unfamiliar (the school restroom, athletic locker room and boiler room). I recall vividly the many sessions that I had with two Junior class gang leaders in my school that were creating a number of problems for staff and students. I decided to meet them on their turf in an attempt to establish some kind of workable relationship. Turf, I unfortunately found, was one of the boys' restrooms some distance from the principal's office. I made it a weekly practice to visit this particular restroom when I knew that the two boys would be present. Non-specific discussions were held with these two youth sitting on the cold tile floor near a bank of white porcelain urinals. At times, I would almost gag from the smell of the urine mixed with stale tobacco smoke. As might be expected, it was impossible to catch the smokers because there was always some student stationed outside the bathroom door to sound a warning if a teacher or school administrator were approaching.

As time passed, I actually began to enjoy our conversations as the process of gaining information and communicating ideas became easier and more open. I found too, that the two young men became individuals with unique personalities rather than two stereotyped antisocial gang leaders. On one occasion, I casually remarked that the cold floor was tough on an old man of 35 and that if they felt so inclined, I would be happy to talk to them in my office. Later, I informed my secretary that if they ever came by for any reason to make sure that I was informed immediately. It took three weeks for this to happen, and when it did I thought that my secretary had just witnessed a near-death experience. She came into my office, a look of apprehension on her face, and with a low, urgent voice motioned to the door, "They're here!" She repeated, "They're here!" Fortunately, I had no one in the office at the time so they were invited in and, as expected, they had come with some complaint to register about the school. Their visits became more frequent and the boys' restroom trips less necessary. Much to my relief, the "ice" was broken and the jagged edges of our relationship as "cop" versus "we guys" began to dissolve. Our friendship grew and I experienced some fine understandings of these youths as we learned how to communicate and trust each other. I was pleased to see gang membership dissolve in the school over a period of months and the two leaders told me if any of the old gang members caused any trouble at the school to let them know. This effort supports some views of communication as a means of creating positive organizational change even in small segments of the system. Although I started the interaction with the two gang leaders as an attempt to change them, I found myself also changing perspective and behavior. As the three of us exchanged information and ideas, we began to understand each other and to appreciate the personal aspects of our being. It is difficult to remain distant and suspicious when senders and receivers are locked together in a mutual bond and open dialogue that permit information to flow freely and without constraints.

To the school administrator, information is a unique resource, and the flow of ideas should be encouraged from all parties in the organization. As Wheatley emphasizes, "For a system to remain alive, for the universe to move onward, information must be continually generated" (p. 104). There is nothing more exciting, motivating and thought provoking than to receive new information. Of course, no one likes to be on the "last one to know" list, so information giving needs to be timely and directed to the right individuals. Above all, to be the most nourishing and rewarding, information needs to be positive, supportive and friendly. It is not pleasant to be around those who constantly complain that life is unbearable, that the school is going downhill, or that kids aren't as smart as they used to be. This is one of the reasons that many consultants at in-service workshops for improving interpersonal relationships typically remind the participants to say three good things about a person for every one criticism. Individuals have a hard time feeling comfortable with discomforts. A lack of interaction, messages that are ambiguous or discomforting, or communication that is too complex tends to be discouraging. Ideal communication must involve a sharing (giving and taking) and some personal interaction. Principals need to be aware that even a smile, warmly and sincerely given, can have very positive and supportive meaning to others. Wheatley (p. 110) refers to the personal aspect of communication by indicating that "we must directly touch what we seek to affect." The school principal has a role to play in the school, and that is shaping the behavior of others. What are some of the ways that the school leader can shape behavior and be an influence in the school? Answers to this question are numerous and often depend upon the setting and the characteristics of the individuals in the organization. In most instances, you can influence others by considering the following points:

- Individuals tend to do those things that get approval. Approval is best given personally in a face-to-face encounter.
- The more information that two individuals hold in common and the more frequent the opportunity for communication, the more likely that the two will interact and find agreement on ideas and proposals.
- There are many levels of communication—the principal should use them all and be conscious of their impact upon others.
- The effective principal will be conscious of the expectations that others have of his or her role and responsibilities and will use that knowledge to meet the needs of others.

Finally, it must be accepted that even good things occasionally break down, and at times, they seem to be in constant need of repair. Breaks in communication are more often the rule than the exception. At times, it is simply necessary to keep communication problems in perspective and to accept some of the following light-hearted occurrences.

FIGURE 1.1. RULES OF COMMUNICATION

- If communication can fail, it most often will.
- If a message can be understood in a number of different ways, it will be understood in just the way that does the most harm.
- There is always someone, or even a lot of people who know better than you what you meant by your message.
- The less communication there is, the more communication that will be generated by those in the organization who are worried about the lack of communication.
- There is always a secretary or administrative assistant who feels that they could have said it better than you did.
- The ideas and comments traveling through the grapevine are most often more interesting and believable than those sent through the regular communication channels.

SUMMARY

Communication is a two-way process that requires effort, skill and sharing by both the sender and receiver. The principal will at times assume each of these roles during communication, and more than anyone else will be expected to send messages clearly and to listen and give feedback in an appropriate manner.

Sincerity and empathy for others increases the chance that communication will be successful. Ideally, each interaction moment should involve sharing and some personal form of interaction. Being personal involves a knowledge of the other person's interests and needs, attempting to look at things from the other person's point of view, paying attention when someone else is speaking and expressing appreciation for the comments given by the speaker.

LEADERSHIP

The primary task of being a leader is to reduce the amount of variation and diverse thinking within the school system. To bring the staff together requires constant communication and frequent face-to-face interaction. Improve your leadership skills by applying these ideas.

- Plan to reserve at least 30 minutes each day to walk around and informally talk to teachers, students and staff.
- Establish a regular communication network (newsletter, faculty meetings, bulletin news board, student of the month photo wall, etc.) to let everyone know what is happening at school.
- Conduct a survey with your staff on the type and amount of information that they would like to receive from you.
- Mix media strategies for variety. Communication to staff might involve small and large group presentations, written notes on specially prepared stationary, newsletters, e-mail, etc.

BIBLIOGRAPHY

Bohn, D., (1980). *Wholeness and the Implicate Order*. London, England: Ark Paperbacks. p. 56.

Doud, J., (1991). "The K–8 Principal in 1988." *National Association of Elementary School Principals, Proficiencies for Principals*. Revised. Alexandria, VA. p. 6–12.

Lemmick, M., (1995). "Glimpses of the Mind." *Time* (July) 146,#3. pp. 48–49.

Martin, W., and Willower, D., (1981). "The Magical Behavior of High School Principals." *Educational Administration Quarterly, 17*. pp. 69–90.

Wheatley, M., (1992). *Leadership and the New Science*. San Francisco: Berrett-Koehler Publishers, Inc. p. 105.

2

THE PROCESS OF COMMUNICATION

There is one thing worse than not communicating: it is thinking that you have communicated when you have not. —Edgar Dale

Schools are literally a beehive of activity and constant noise. In place of the hum of machinery in the large factory, the noise of schools is that of interaction. Teaching and learning involves talking and listening. The communication process, as most people are aware, is simply that of individuals sending and receiving messages in order to be understood. Communication is simple to describe or illustrate, but very difficult to implement in a satisfying and effective manner with any degree of regularity and clarity (Daresh and Playko, 1995).

DID YOU HEAR WHAT I SAID?

The simple act of communication, as observed in Figure 2.1, involves a sender (for the purpose of this discussion, the principal) giving an oral message, to a receiver (who could be a teacher, secretary, student, etc.).

FIGURE 2.1

The expectation is that the listener will accept the message as it was accurately given and respond as the sender expects. But, as most people are aware, communication is really more complex than simple. The difficulty with accuracy is getting messages across to others, especially in an organizational setting where interaction is vitally important to effectiveness and productivity, is that more than verbal exchanges are involved.

When a message is given, complex interaction between the sender and receiver is at play. Personality factors, such as participant intellect, emotional and physical well-being, feelings and attitudes, interests, role responsibilities and motivation, to name a few, color or distort messages. For example, take this dialogue between a mother and her five year old daughter. The mother is busily preparing the evening dinner and checking the progress of her daughter who is picking up toys left in the playroom. In another room, baby Robert is crying, wanting to be picked up and nurtured after taking a nap. The mother, with her arms covered with flour and bread dough cannot immediately respond to the baby's needs. She remarks in an exasperated manner, speaking out loud to herself, "That baby is spoiled rotten! He could lie there quietly for a few minutes without fussing—what he needs is a good spanking!"

Within seconds, the mother hears her daughter remark angrily to Robert, "Bad baby! What you need is a good spanking!" The sounds of slapping reach her ears as well as the increased volume and frequency of cries from Robert. The mother rushes into the nursery and finds her daughter spanking (with little physical damage) baby Robert. "What are you doing?" The mother asks questioningly. The daughter responds, "You said that Robert needs a good spanking, so I am helping you." "Oh dear," the mother retorts warmly and picks up the baby and then pats her daughter on the head, "I only said that Robert needs a spanking because I was busy. I didn't really mean that Robert needs a spanking." Then, looking kindly to her daughter, she instructs, "I know that you were trying to help, but in the future, remember that only mother can spank Robert, but you can always help me take care of him." What has happened in this familiar home setting? The verbal message was simple and clear to the daughter.

However, she had not, at such a young age, learned the role relationships in a family that differentiate among the responsibilities of a mother and that of a daughter. She is also in the process of learning that what you hear is not always to be taken literally. The mother has also learned something new in the communication process—to be cautious in what is said around her daughter who is not quite old enough to reason through the complexities of language and meaning.

Because messages may be interpreted differently than expected, Figure 2.2 illustrates the possible influence of receiver attitudes, experiences, concerns and personality traits upon communication accuracy.

FIGURE 2.2

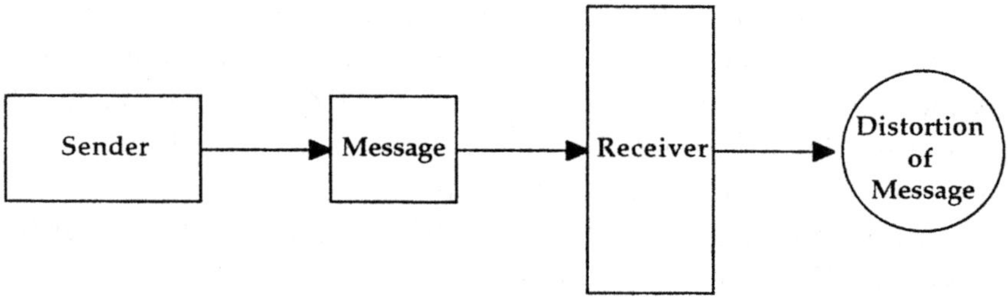

In Figure 2.2, the sender has a message to send. In this instance, the sender may be very certain about the message's clarity and intent, but the receiver's perception of the message may vary considerably. As has been mentioned, feelings and attitudes, prior experiences with the sender, the time of day, peer relationships, role power, etc. can influence or distort a message. The complexity of this interplay may be illustrated in a typical school situation where a principal meets one of the teachers walking in the hallway. The principal speaks first, "Hi Jane, I was just going to your classroom. I want to remind you of the curriculum meeting today after school. We need to start right at 3:30—as soon as your last class is over. Is that okay with you?"

The teacher slows her pace, nods her head indicating that she has heard the message and replies with some distress splashing quickly across her face, "It is difficult to collect my materials, lock up the classroom and get to the meeting on time, but I will try." She averts her gaze from the principal and nervously walks on in an obvious hurry.

The message from the principal and the response from the teacher are simple and clearly stated in context, but not necessarily so in feeling. The principal has picked up some feedback in the worried look on the teacher's face and her eye avoidance as they walked by each other. The teacher is very concerned about the chance meeting in the hallway and interaction with the principal. As she continues walking toward her destination, lines of tension wrinkle her forehead. These thoughts tumble through her mind in rapid sequence:

"I leave my classroom for five minutes and who do I meet, the principal! I'm sure he now thinks that I leave my room, with students unsupervised, whenever I please."

"I get sick of him walking the hallways to see who is in class and who isn't. Doesn't he have other things to do?"

"He doesn't know that I am worried about my 10 year old son who is home alone with a fever of 101 degrees. It is so hard to teach school full-time and raise a family too. The principal's children are all raised, and he wouldn't understand that I told my son I would call every hour to see how he was feeling."

"I have been so worried about my son's illness that I completely forgot about that meeting. I need to be home, not discussing the 4th grade curriculum for two hours. The principal calls too many meetings on short notice. I wish that he would be more considerate of teacher responsibilities."

"I wonder what he meant by stressing the 3:20 p.m. starting time? He sounded sarcastic. I have only been late for these meetings the last two times. Why doesn't he ask the teachers when they would like to meet?"

The teacher sighs and mutters, "This day is starting out very badly."

Few messages are sent without some form of feedback taking place. Feedback or message acknowledgment may be in the form of a verbal response, a physical cue (such as a nod or facial expression) or both. Feedback is also a message—coming from the receiver. The sender looks for feedback and uses this information to determine if his or her message was received as desired (see Fig. 2.3).

FIGURE 2.3

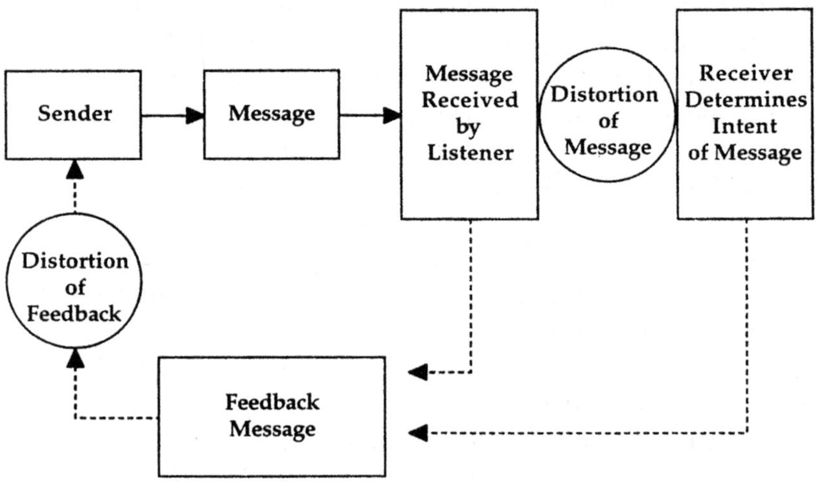

It must be remembered that immediate feedback will not always reflect the listeners' true or ultimate feelings about a message. Often, acknowledgment of a message is given and an interaction terminated, without much time or thought being given to the meanings behind the sender's comments. Thus, in the principal/teacher interaction just mentioned, the principal knows that the message was received, but is not really sure how it was received by the teacher.

The teacher's response to the principal in this instance also left the administrator with some thoughts about the interaction. The principal may have noted the nervous look on the teacher's face and her reluctance to stop or look at him directly. For certain, he will reflect upon her reason for leaving a classroom full of students. He may also wonder if his added comment about the 3:30 p.m. meeting time being okay with her was a little too pointed. After all, she had been late to the previous two meetings. But he is well aware from their interactions over the years that this teacher is very sensitive and can easily become distressed. As a wise administrator, this principal will realize that it will be necessary to interact with the teacher again soon to make sure that the relationship remains positive and cordial and that he becomes aware of any home or school difficulties that the teacher may be having.

Leadership is an art and one of the qualities of artful leadership is having a sensitivity to the concerns and needs of others. Experienced and caring principals know that it is not a forceful personality, a strong voice or the power of the position that motivates and inspires others to do their best. In short, as Max DePree (1989) indicates, the true leader is a listener. The leader is always listening for and observing indications of other's needs, aspirations and concerns. When it is apparent that communication may be awry, the leader reconsiders the message that was given, its possible impact upon the system of beliefs of others, possible distortions that may occur and then responds in the most appropriate manner. The responsibility of the administrator is to help others do their jobs to the best of their abilities. To do this requires clear thinking and awareness of possible causes of message distortion.

MESSAGE BARRIERS

Those who study communication among humans recognize that the most complex part of the process is understanding what we are saying to one another. It may be that others have different meanings for the words that we used, or it may be that they were not even interested in what we were saying. The so called "breakdowns in communication" are to be expected and the reasons for these problems are often referred to as communication barriers. It should be no surprise when it becomes apparent that a message has been misunderstood. Each message that is received has meanings attached to it from the personal experience base of each individual. It is relatively easy to see the evidence of communication such as the expressions of the interactants, the words, the symbols, the media materials used, etc., but not so easy to observe below the surface barriers that may arise. It is difficult to determine, for instance, how personal pressures, moods, attitudes and self-concepts will impact upon the message. Communication is a human activity, and the principal must be prepared to understand the large invisible barriers that make communication either work or become difficult. Some of the more common barriers to good communication are filtering, information overload, status or role differences, and stereotyping. An understanding of each of these potential communication modifiers will assist the principal in better understanding how messages are received or distorted.

FILTERING

A filter is a device used to screen out or remove substances that are considered undesirable or lacking in value. Filtering, in communication, involves only reporting or giving parts of information knowledge to a receiver. Often, the reason for a partial message is that the entire volume of information on the subject is too complex, detailed, negative in intent, or involves some personal information that should be held in confidence or that might offend the receiver. The principal often has the more complete information on a problem or school situation and must determine how much of this information to give to others. For instance, suppose that a parent has called about the behavior of a teacher in class. It has been reported to the parent by one of her children that the teacher in question is permitting students to play a "slug on the shoulder game" the first five minutes of the class period. The parent reports that her son has been complaining of a sore arm and is frightened about going to class. She wants the activity stopped, but does not want her son's name given to the teacher. The parent asks the principal if other parents had complained about this questionable activity. The principal has received two other complaints, but feels that it would be potentially dangerous to give this information to the parent at this time. Upon questioning the teacher, the principal discovers that this activity has been taking place during the week. The teacher reports that the students voted to do this as part of a class planning activity in which they are involved. The principal advises the teacher to stop the activity and explains the dangers of allowing students to hit one another. The teacher agrees, but asks the principal how he found out that the activity was taking place. The principal, upon considering all aspects of the situation and the information received, may decide to filter some of the message that is given to the teacher.

Filtering out difficult or unpleasant messages is troublesome to the principal. There is always a concern that if names are given of those who are involved in a problem, that some hostility or anger might be aroused. Potentially unpleasant messages should be given with care and consideration for all involved. If it is possible to speak frankly without passing names, this should be done. However, the principal should be careful to not filter out too much of a message in attempting to soften the criticism or concern regarding the behavior of others. As difficult as it may be, messages that offer constructive criticism need to be given and need to be listened to with attention and care. It is important that teachers, students, staff members, etc. have the opportunity to examine the assumptions about schooling and relationships and to compare those assumptions with the values and expectations of the principal and school system.

Research has shown that many administrators are reluctant to transmit negative information downward. Teachers, for instance, are very sensitive about criticisms from the principal because of fear of performance ratings being lowered. There is a tendency for teachers to question seriously any critical reference to teaching performance, knowing that the principal can only be in the classroom a limited period of time during the school year. Thus, the teacher, in many instances, can report to the principal that the information he or she has received is only hearsay or is not correct. It has been found, however, that subordinates who had good performance ratings were more likely to be informed of those ratings than subordinates who had poor ratings (Johns, 1983). It is also a possibility that a marginal teacher may use the positive information to support a claim for continuance of contract because of a record of improvement being on file.

The principal needs to be aware that filtering occurs in an upward flow too. Because principals are in a position to give or withhold rewards to teachers, staff members and students, such filtering will be obvious. Research indicates that subordinates who are upwardly mobile are especially likely to filter information to the leader that is positive. Likewise, those who desire to impress their administrative leader will manipulate unfavorable information about themselves in order to appear capable and supportive (Jublin, 1987).

INFORMATION OVERLOAD

If you check the typical principal's desk, you will discover a number of stacks of papers involving assignments to be completed and a variety of telephone notes indicating individuals that need information and want to be contacted. At times, principals have so much responsibility and work to do that they feel ineffective. As a result of all the information that comes to the principal and the data that must be provided to others, it becomes practically impossible to absorb or adequately respond to all of it, particularly within a 40-hour week. Thus, in order to attempt to keep up, administrators select parts of the information to file, record and distribute, which often results in incomplete or inaccurate information on which to make decisions (Lunenburg & Ornstein, 1991).

Information overload will continue to be a problem for principals because of the increasing complexity of operating the school program. A number of principals are now using computers in their offices to store and retrieve information. However, with the computer, the volume of information and data that are available increases the time that is necessary to sit and relate to the technology. Principals frequently have problems in making the necessary personal contacts with individuals, and sitting before a computer lessens those valuable human encounters. In order to be effective, principals must organize their time and that of their secretaries so that information can be processed, filtered as necessary to exclude less relevant information, and ranked in importance for response.

ROLE AND STATUS DIFFERENCES IN THE SCHOOL

The organization of the school system creates differing job responsibilities and assignments. School districts create status differences through assignments of job titles, work responsibilities, information channels, salary recommendations and policy regulations. As much as a principal may want to relate closely to teachers, students, staff and parents, and expect and receive open communication, the status of the position will interfere with the free flow of information. It is common for teachers who are elevated to positions of administration in a school to notice a change in how they are accepted and treated by their former peers. In many instances the communications pattern becomes more formed, less frequent and topics of discussion are more limited.

The more that a subordinate is removed from an administrator through organizational levels of leadership, the increased likelihood exists that communication will be more easily misunderstood. In addition, individuals who are removed from an information source tend to feel less personal involvement, interest and feelings of cohesiveness with the administrative office. Such a communication pattern often exists in large school districts where the superintendent must attempt to communicate effectively to hundreds of teachers located in a number of schools.

THE SCHOOL AS AN INTERACTIVE SYSTEM

Principals must realize that they work in a social system in which the organizational structure places them apart from teachers. Getzels and Guba (1957) refer to this system as the nomothetic or institutional dimension, and the ideographic or individual dimension. As an institution carries out its identified function, it is crucial that certain role responsibilities and organizational expectations be met. In business the bottom line is to sell a desirable product and to make a profit. The school system, too, has a role to perform and expectations to be met. The system employs teachers to instruct students and school administrators to meet other expectations which includes that of staffing, developing school schedules, facilities maintenance, budget control, carrying out state and school district policies, record keeping, student management, etc. These nomothetic or institutional responsibilities, are usually not within the job requirements of teachers and students who have other responsibilities in the school.

Teachers act in certain ways that influence instruction and learning with students. The classroom prescribes a more limited setting for teachers than that of the principal, who has a total school responsibility. The classroom becomes the workplace of teachers and students, and there is an expectation that the school (administrators and support staff) will be available and ready to meet their individual and group needs. Teachers and students have unique personalities and particular needs that often come into conflict with other teachers and even the expectations of the school. Figure 2.4 illustrates the social system model showing the nomothetic and ideographic dimensions and their interactions. Although the model depicts a parallel of alignment of the two dimensions, this does not mean that harmony prevails. As might be expected, in most organizations, unless robots are assuming the functions of the workers, it is impossible to not have conflict and some dysfunctions occur. If the expectations and authority of the institution becomes too powerful, the needs and well-being of the individuals in the organization may suffer, and production

FIGURE 2.4

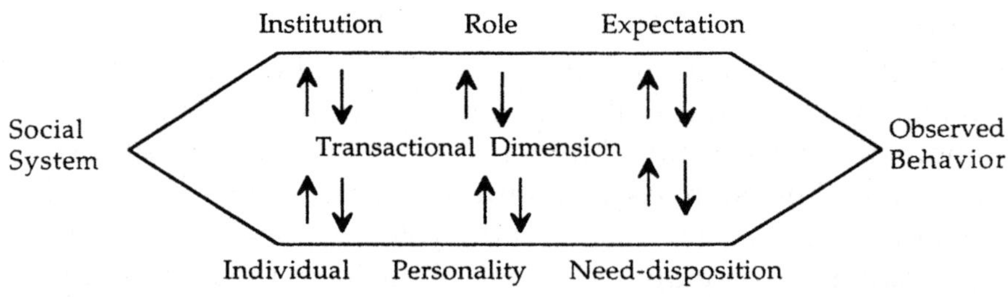

and worker morale decrease. On the other hand, if the wishes and desires of the individuals within the organization become overly excessive and demanding, common goals may disappear, chaos may occur and the institution may fail to meet the expectations to which it was organized. Thus, some type of transactional or intermediate balance is needed so that institution expectations are met and individual needs are fulfilled.

The principal is the person most often considered the one to maintain the proper balance within the school by supporting institutional demands and also meeting human needs of teachers, parents, students and staff members. To do this, the school leader must be able to articulate the purposes of the school (rules, regulations, and goals) and gain the support of teachers, parents and students to meeting the school's missions. While this is occurring the principal must help others to feel important and that they contribute to school performance and student success.

Understanding this model allows the principal to be more effective in his or her assignment. Daresh and Playko (1995), suggest that the principal's role is the process of overseeing the ability of teachers, students and staff to meet the needs and goals of the organization in which they work.

The principal is often caught in the middle, attempting to balance the many expectations of the position and to keep conflicts at a minimum. Role and personality conflicts are the most common of the difficulties faced by school leaders, and those conflicts lead to misunderstandings regarding communication. Teachers view the principal as their supervisor who is willing to donate time and support in helping them to do their jobs well.

As the principal attempts to balance individual requests with the expectations and goals of the total organization, the decisions made may at times be viewed negatively by the teachers. A few examples will illustrate how easy it is for individuals in the organization to disagree or become upset with the decisions of the school leader. Read the five school episode situations carefully and decide if you would choose a more institutional role (concern about the total organization goals and maintaining balance and harmony) or a more individual role (concern that individual teachers feel valuable and are supported in their roles as teacher leaders). After you make a decision, indicate the individual or individuals that might feel that your decision was not a desirable one and not in their best interest or in the best interest of the total school program. How would you communicate to those individuals who are not in harmony with your decision?

FIVE EPISODE SITUATIONS

Instructions: Read each situation and then indicate what decision you would make.

- The music teacher, Ms. Young, is a talented and popular music teacher. She asks you, the principal, if she can have her mixed chorus of 24 students excused for two periods of class once a week for the next six weeks in order to prepare for the school assembly in which the governor of the state will be attending to present a Citation of Excellence to the school. She insists that her choir must have this practice time if they are to be perfect at the assembly. The students will be missing classes in other subjects, but Ms. Young feels that the teachers should be supportive and should agree that the students need the extra practice. During the two extra hours of practice, Ms. Young suggests that she send the students that she has for those two periods (beginning chorus and social studies) to the library with assigned projects to work on. As the principal, what is your decision?

Definitely support the teacher's request	Support, but with concerns about the attitudes of the teachers and parents	Reject the teacher's request, but offer some alternatives	Reject the teacher's request and cite disruption of school programs as a factor

Is your decision school goals oriented or more concerned about the needs of the individual? ________________

____

Who will probably be upset with your decision and why?

____

____

- Mr. Jabar is a second year teacher, and is very enthusiastic and liked by the students. He comes to you and requests that he be permitted to use a different literature book than is being used by the other four English teachers who teach at the same grade level. Mr. Jabar indicates that the book that he wants to use is far superior to the other one and that his book (approved by the state textbook adoption committee) contains numerous entries from authors of various countries and cultures. The other English teachers feel that it is not necessary to change texts, especially when the set being used is only four years old. You do have the money to buy a set of the new books for Mr. Jabar if you choose to do so. However, there are other teachers in the school who have requested text changes, too, who may also request money for new books. As the principal, what is your decision?

Definitely support the teacher	Support, but with concerns about the attitude of other teachers	Indicate no, but suggest some possible changes in the future	Definitely indicate no to the request and cite school policy and levels of department approval

Is your decision nomothetic or ideographic directed?

____

____

Who might be upset with your decision and why?

____

____

- Mr. Black and Mrs. Johnson, from the mathematics department, come to you with a class change proposal. Mr. Black wants to switch classes with Mrs. Johnson's fourth period so that he can teach the advanced calculus class and Mrs. Johnson can teach the basic math class. Both teachers favor the change because Mrs. Johnson does not feel as confident with higher math. However, this change will give Mr. Black all of his classes with the better math students and Mrs. Johnson will have all of the more remedial classes. As the principal, you have always preferred that teachers share in teaching courses to students with differing abilities. This request will be in line with what Mr. Black has wanted for the last two years, as he has not been interested in teaching lower ability students. If you approve, some of the other teachers may want to switch classes, too. As the principal, what is your decision?

Strongly support the change	Support the change, but with concerns	Not support the change, but indicate that it might be possible in the future	Strongly reject the change and give reasons

Is your decision nomothetic or ideographic directed?

____

____

Who might be upset with your decision and why?

____

____

- A group of parents who support clogging groups in town come to you with a request that students have an opportunity to be taught popular dances during school time. They suggest that this could be done in P.E. classes once or twice a month for a class period. They present to you a parent's support form, signed by 100 parents in the community. The group has even found a retired teacher who will do the teaching free. The group will donate the music tapes to the school. You tell the group that you will get back with them as soon as you talk to the teachers in the P.E. department. Upon checking with the school district, you are told that this type of activity is approved if supervised by the P.E. teachers. However, your P.E. teachers are reluctant to agree because they feel that the activity will infringe upon the regular curricular program planned for the students. They feel that dancing should be extracurricular and not sponsored by the school. As the principal, what is your decision?

Strongly support the parents	Support the parents on a trial basis	Not allow the dance activity but suggest other solutions	Disapprove the request because of the many problems that may occur

Is your decision nomothetic or ideographic oriented?

____

Who might be upset with your decision and why?

____

____

- Mr. Mendez, the Spanish teacher, has been taking a group of students each year on a trip to Mexico during the spring break in April. He comes to you with a request to extend the trip an extra week because of the extensive travel time and the increased opportunity to stay in homes of the citizens and learn more about the culture and depth. You are aware that the money for the trip comes from the parents at no cost to the school. The teachers in the school will probably support a decision to let Mr. Mendez have the students miss a week of school because they are all top students in advanced Spanish classes. On the other hand, only 30% of the parents in Mr. Mendez's classes can afford the trip, leaving a number of students to stay at school and be taught by a substitute teacher. Some parents have complained that Mr. Mendez operates an elitist program for the wealthy students. Mr. Mendez says that if he cannot have the extra week, he will cancel the trip entirely because it is too much work for him to only go for two weeks. As the principal, what is your decision?

You support the extra week	You support the extra week, but indicate that the issue will be reviewed after this trip	You deny the request, but indicate that you will review the trip plan and extra days during the year	You deny the request and indicate that there are too many difficulties with having students gone from school for an extra week

Who might be upset with your decision and why? ___

___

Upon examination of each episode, it is apparent that regardless of the decision made by the principal, someone will be upset. In each instance, the school administrator must be sensitive to the concerns of the people in the organization, but also be aware of how decisions will impact the effectiveness of the total school program (nomothetic dimension). It is important that the principal be aware that with the position go certain responsibilities that cannot be abrogated.

MAINTAINING HARMONY IN THE SCHOOL

The primary purpose of the principal's job is to carry out state and school policy, to maintain harmony in the school, to ensure that students are receiving a quality education and that conflicts are handled fairly and expediently. Through the use of communication skills, the principal can reduce conflict by:

- Keeping the teachers, students and parents informed of school policy and legal responsibilities for certain school activities and functions.
- Maintaining a constant interaction with staff, faculty and students to articulate beliefs, to explain and defend decisions and to review role responsibilities.
- Expressing disagreement without being disagreeable or defensive. Disagreements will invariably arise, and a calm

and decisive manner will always be respected even if the decision rendered is not a favorable one.

- Utilizing all the information that is available when making decisions that may be disagreeable to others. The principal should use active listening skills to gain information and better understand differing points of view.
- Realizing that there may be more than one competing argument for what should be done, with each proponent equally convinced that their version is the best one. It is wisdom to realize that what seems logical to one person may appear folly to another. In these instances, it is useful for the principal to listen to all points of view, to present his or her solution rationally and understandably and to arrive at solutions that are satisfying to most of the participants.

Conflict is an expected part of organizational life. It is not possible for the principal to be everything to everyone. The school leader needs to know how to work with conflict and to realize that the role of principal brings with it certain expectations from others. As conflicts or disagreements within the school arise, the principal needs to decide if the needs of the individual can be met or if a decision needs to be made that is in line with the expectations of the institution. It is important that the principal continually assess personal goals and objectives for the school to see how these values are guiding actions and behavior. By reviewing personal principles and prior decisions, it will be possible to determine if you are maintaining a balance between institutional expectations and individual needs.

Without question, it is essential that administration be socially perceptive of their relationship with others if they are to minimize conflicts. The unique task of the administrator is to integrate the requirements of the institution and the desires of the staff members in a way that is organizationally productive and individually satisfying. Often, the administrator must be willing to place personal interests and needs secondary to that of assisting the individuals in the school to be fulfilled in their positions and to work harmoniously with others toward mutually acceptable goals.

School administrators often become so busy that they appear to be withholding needed information, are indifferent to the needs of others and in some instances, are even arrogant. These perceptions strengthen status differentials by causing the administrator to be less open to feedback or other forms of communication (Lunenburg & Ornstein, 1991).

FIVE REASONS TO COMMUNICATE

School principals must communicate for five very important reasons. These are to inform, persuade, influence the actions of others, strengthen relationships, and gain information.

- Informing is a very important part of the principal's school responsibility. Nothing creates more difficulty in a school than inadequate information coming from the school leader. The image that the principal projects is often formed by how well he or she articulates beliefs, explains decisions, clarifies rules and regulations, responds to issues, informs others of programs and accomplishments, and honestly and openly communicates.
- The principal must be able to persuade others to consider and accept the school's philosophy, mission, needs and actions toward improvement. To do this, the principal must know how to negotiate well, to present new ideas, to involve others and to sincerely value their input and suggestions. Persuasion isn't the art of forcing one's will upon others. An essential ingredient of persuasion is knowing what you are talking about, but realizing that you cannot know everything, and that the ideas of others will also contribute to the effectiveness of the school organization. True leadership is primarily thinking that we, as an organization, are changing and improving and not that I have initiated changes in others that will help them improve.
- Many of the decisions that occur in the school setting come from the joint efforts of the principal, teachers, students,

parents and staff. In addition to being persuasive, the principal must be able to influence the actions of others who work in groups or committees. Work groups in the school often require the school leader to provide direction, motivation, and influence, to assist the members in resolving problems and effectively attaining delegated responsibilities. In this regard, the school administrator must be able to articulate group responsibilities clearly and effectively.

- Strengthening relationships is a process of encouraging others to feel successful at school in their personal development and in their social interactions with others. The principal needs to model inviting and accepting behavior, as well as encourage others to exhibit such behavior. Good leadership is the process of inviting teachers, staff members and students to see themselves as able, valuable, self-directing and able to act in accordance with these positive perceptions (Purkey and Novak, 1984).
- Lastly, information collection is vital to the work of the principal. Good decisions and reactions to situations are difficult to make without adequate information. I often reflect on the successful campaigns of great military leaders such as General Napoleon Bonaparte, the Emperor of France from 1804–1815, Thomas "Stonewall" Jackson, the Confederate general during the Civil War, and General Dwight D. Eisenhower, a World War II leader and the 34th President of the United States. Each of these leaders spent the necessary time collecting facts and even exposed themselves to danger in order to receive the most reliable information. Once they had collected the information that best described the situation facing them they were able to make decisive decisions at critical points in military campaigns. All of us who have served or are serving as school administrators are accustomed to making decisions. In some instances, prior experience is all that is necessary to resolve a problem; while in other situations, information collection is necessary if the most appropriate decisions are to be made. Some of the advantages of personally

contacting individuals for information regarding a situation are evident. It is often an advantage to contact others to slow down the decision making process and to see if there are gaps in the information you have received that are not immediately apparent. The very process of information gathering also displays your interest in what others have to contribute and helps them to feel a part of the decision making process.

Within the school, department chairs, committee members, custodians, student leaders and teachers with specialized skills also possess important information and may be utilized to gather information. As a result of their knowledge and positions of influence in the communication network, they can contribute considerably in the decision making process.

THE SETTING

As has been mentioned, the messages that are sent and received will be distorted depending on the biases, prejudices, erroneous assumptions, attitudes and mental set of the receiver. In addition, interactions that take place with others are affected by at least three other dimensions. Devito (1988) refers to these components as the physical context, the socio-psychological dimension and the temporal setting.

Communication always takes place somewhere, and for the principal, school interactions usually occur in the office, hallway, school grounds or classrooms. The environment will often dictate the nature and the level of seriousness of a message. The principal, for instance, would not likely want to discuss a teacher's classroom performance at a school dance or in the hallway. Likewise, an invitation to meet with the principal in his or her office will usually be considered a very serious occasion by a student or parent.

The social-psychological dimension of communication includes the relationships among the individuals interacting, the roles assigned or played by group members, the norms and cultural context of the school and the type of social situations in which interactions occur. As an example, students would expect the principal to be less formal and more friendly at an after school function (dance, game, play, etc.) than during school hours. Teachers would also look for more humor and light-heartedness from the principal at a faculty picnic or a pre-school breakfast than they would at a faculty meeting or committee work session.

The time of day is considered as part of the temporal setting. For a number of individuals, the morning hours are not a good time for communication of a serious and involved nature. For others, afternoon meetings may be challenging and tiring because they are seemingly more alert and ready to complete tasks in the morning hours. Some teachers like to arrive at school an hour early to get started on school planning and, unfortunately, they like the principal to be there also to answer questions. Other teachers prefer to do their planning after school, and likewise want the principal available for support. In these instances, the principal must decide upon a reasonable work schedule and communicate clearly his or her best hours for work and interaction so as not to be overwhelmed by the number of hours that need to be maintained at school. I recall an occasion when it was necessary for me to complete a lengthy accreditation report at the university. I thought that if I came into my office at 5:30 a.m. every morning for a couple of weeks that I would have some uninterrupted time and be able to complete the report on schedule. I didn't realize that one of the faculty had been coming to school at that terribly early hour for years. As a result, he would stop by the office every morning between 5:30 and 6:00 a.m. to chat. Needless to say, I had to come up with another work plan in order to complete the report.

Another important dimension of time refers to how a message that is given fits into a sequence of history or communication events. For instance, a teacher telling students that she is giving a "pop quiz" will receive different student responses if the message is given on a regular school day, or on a Friday before the event of a "big game" with a rival school. Likewise, the principal who asks a teacher to serve on a school committee may receive a varied response, depending upon the attitude of the teacher toward previous committee assignments and how valuable the teacher felt the results were in resolving important school issues.

SUMMARY

Principals are in constant contact with many others during the school day to accomplish the mission of the school. Many of these contacts involve sending and receiving messages. During school, messages are used to coordinate the work of the faculty and staff, and to facilitate student good behavior and learning. In most instances, messages are sent and communication occurs with the sender and receiver expecting the interaction to be positive and the messages to be clearly stated and understood. However, the feelings and attitudes of the sender and receiver, the time of day, role relationships, the nature of the message, etc., can influence or distort a message. It is difficult for the sender of a message to always determine how personal pressures, moods and self-concepts will impact a message. The school principal must be aware of communication barriers and understand that the communication, even under the best of circumstances, may be received differently than expected. A few of the most common barriers to good communication are filtering, information overload, status or role differences, overinterpretation of messages and stereotyping.

School principals must communicate frequently to inform others about school happenings and to gain information that will support decision making. Additional reasons for communication involve the need to influence others to take particular actions and to strengthen relationships. The very process of communication by the principal displays an interest in what others have to contribute, recognizes the value of the individual, and supports the decision making process as a group responsibility. Oral communication is an active process. The principal needs to communicate in order to make connections with others, to "know about" what is happening at school and to make sure that information is being as accurately conveyed as possible.

TEACHER INSERVICE

Institute a vigorous program of education and professional development for your staff. Doing so improves faculty morale and lets the staff members know that you are interested in their professional growth.

Consider these ideas:

- Plan and provide funds for at least three faculty members each semester to attend some workshop or meeting that will improve their skill in school management, group dynamics, decision making, program evaluation, etc.
- Provide time for faculty members to report their attendance at meetings and workshops to the entire faculty. Also write up faculty inservice activities and include in school and district newsletter to parents.
- Plan on taking faculty members with you to certain conferences and workshops that you attend during the year. Togetherness during a trip builds trust, support and openness that is valuable in running an effective school.
- Conduct a faculty meeting or workshop on the importance of positive communication to parents and community members. Discuss ways that communication channels can be opened and the types of information that needs to be sent to parents.

BIBLIOGRAPHY

Daresh, J., & Playko, M., (1995). *Supervision as a Proactive Process: Concepts and Cases*. Prospect Heights, IL: Waveland Press, Inc. p. 164.

DePree, M. (1989). *Leadership is an Art*. (p. xxi). New York: Dell Publishing Co. p. 131.

Devito, J., (1988). *Human Communication: The Basic Course (4th ed.)*. New York: Harper & Row, Publishers.

Jablin, F. et al., eds. (1987). *Handbook or Organizational Communication*. Newberry Park, CA: Sage.

Johns, G. (1983). *Organizational Behavior: Understanding Life at Work*. Glenview, IL: Scott Foresman.

Lunenburg, F., & Ornstein, A., (1991). *Educational Administration: Concepts and Practices*. Belmont, CA: Wadsworth Publishing Co. p. 204.

Purkey, W., & Novak, J. (1984). *Inviting School Success: A Self-Concept Approach to Teaching and Learning*. Belmont, CA: Wadsworth Publishing Co. p. iii.

3

Understanding and Using Nonverbal Behavior

Sherlock Holmes to Dr. Watson: "You see but you do not observe."

Nonverbal communication has received considerable attention during the past few years as a result of extensive study and some revealing facts about the influence of nonverbal behavior. The spoken word is most often used to convey language, but much of the information involved in the process comes from nonverbal or body language. Some estimates place well over half of all information that is given in day-to-day interaction as being nonverbal.

Body movements and gestures during speaking often convey more information than the words. For instance, if you are talking to someone and they yawn, or their eyes begin to glance at other objects such as their watch or the window, what is your reaction? Do you continue to talk without noticing the behavior, or do you begin to think, "This person is not interested in what I am saying," or "I had better terminate my discussion as this person seems anxious to do something else." You may even think that the other person is rude, especially if you assumed that your comments are very important and need the other person's full attention. In any event, even though the individual may make no comment about the time and a need to complete some tasks, you will probably close the conversation as soon as possible and leave.

Nonverbal language can often speak louder than what is said verbally. I recall a dinner invitation a few years back at the home of a very well-to-do patron of the school district in which I was a high school principal. This was a neighborhood dinner and social event designed for the public to meet the new principal and his wife. Because of school delays I was late by 15 minutes which is a "no! no!" in any situation, but especially at a home in which a maid answers the door and the dinner is prepared by the host's personal chef. The maid promptly opened the door upon my knock, and we were greeted at the steps leading to the front room by the hostess. Her welcome was socially correct and gracious as she stated, "Dr. Muse and Mrs. Muse, it is so good that you could come," as she gave a quick smile, but the rest of her facial features told another story. Her eyes narrowed and her pupils appeared small and piercing as she studied my face. I could detect muscle tension around the jaw area, and I knew that she wasn't pleased with my late arrival. The dinner went well, however, and I attempted to be a very social and pleasant school principal to the group. As the evening progressed, the hostess seemed to become much more at ease, and she even smiled a couple of times in my direction with a much more relaxed and forgiving demeanor.

The use of the body through facial expressions, posture, hand and arm gestures, vocal tone, pitch and distance between those interacting can reinforce or detract from the intent of the spoken language. Body movements communicate one's thoughts and feelings accurately and often consistently (Devito, 1988). People in depression or in stressful situations will often exhibit the same behavioral mannerisms over an extended period of time. Also, those who know us well are quick to notice a sudden change in behavior or bearing. On these occasions, friends might ask, "Are you feeling well, your face doesn't look so good," or "Get those shoulders back, the football team's loss can't be that bad!" Notice too, that when individuals speak who are tired or stressed, their vitality drops, the speech slows down and the pitch of the voice drops considerably. Sudden unusual changes in nonverbal behavior often is an indication of an emotional and attitude change.

One of the most important functions of nonverbal movement is its role in influencing the perceptions and feelings of others. Sometimes referred to as illustrators, there are physical cues that are used to directly support the spoken words (Ekman & Friesen, 1972). The comment, "I am pleased with your work on that committee," followed by a smile reinforces the statement. The speaker who remarks, "Let's think about this problem and see if we can come up with some possible solutions," as she points to her temple with a forefinger, is visually indicating to others that she is open to ideas and wants some serious thinking on the subject.

At times, body movements can speak for themselves without any verbal cues. A smile is always a positive gesture, and, included with a wink or thumbs up, can signify "That's done well," "I agree with you," or "Keep up the good work." It is possible that a speaker can say something and, unknowingly, give a physical cue (a furrowed brow, a hand to chin as if worried, or folded arms, etc.) that is random and not meant to give any particular meaning. When this occurs, the speaker, looking intently at the listener, may think that a physical cue has been given, and that the listener is questioning a proposal or idea. The speaker may even comment, "I can see by your frown that you are not in agreement with my idea." The listener may seem surprised that the speaker had picked up such a meaning, and hurriedly remark, "Oh, no! I like your idea. I was just thinking through how others who would be involved would respond."

The school principal should be aware that when giving a message and using nonverbal cues, the listener may become confused if the cues and spoken comments are not supportive. Thus, a habitual glance at your wrist watch or a shuffling of paper on the desk might be interpreted by a visitor as a signal that you are busy, pressed for time, or that the meeting must end soon. As people interact, they are giving nonverbal cues, and, simultaneously, these cues are being observed by each participant in an attempt to determine what the other is thinking and feeling.

There are three major forms of nonverbal behaviors that accompany and supplement language. The three areas with related subgroups are:

- *Paralanguage*
  Voice loudness
  Speed of speaking
  Tone of voice
- *Body language*
  Appearance
  Facial signals
  Gestures
- *Space*
  Personal
  Touching
  Physical environment

Each one of these areas will be discussed and their importance in the process of communication explained.

PARALANGUAGE

The way that an individual uses language can say as much about the person as the words and sentences uttered. Paralanguage consists of nonverbal voice cues that accompany speech. The speaker's loudness, speed of speech, pitch of voice, tone or emphasis on words, and inflection give added meaning to the spoken words. Even stuttering, whimpering, yawning and giggling give the observer impressions of the speaker and the intent of the message. A few people stutter when they become nervous or feel strongly about some issue being discussed. Giggling can also occur as a result of being nervous or in attempting to suppress a full laugh about something considered funny or entertaining. A "slip of the tongue" comment can create a laughing situation that shouldn't be considered as negative unless the laughter is at someone's expense and they are made to feel foolish.

Paralanguage is often overemphasized in telephone conversations because the speaker is not able to use body movements to emphasize meaning. As a person speaks, the listener attempts to determine the feelings and emotional levels being expressed. In the following examples, consider the expressions from listeners as they attempt to respond to paralanguage cues:

- "I don't like the tone of your voice."
- "I know it's important, you don't have to shout."
- "Are you serious or just kidding?"
- "You sure are in a bad mood today."
- "Are you asking or telling me to do that?"

When a speaker uses loudness, the intent may be to emphasize a point, gain attention, stress some action or indicate a desire to be included in a discussion. Pitch is useful in determining if a sentence is a statement, question or a sarcastic barb. For instance, the phrase, "Are you ready to go?" can be merely a statement of readiness, a question of preparedness, or a teasing statement sarcastically indicating that it is a known fact for the individual to usually be late and seldom ready on time.

Speed in speech is used when a speaker wishes to be more persuasive or to emphasize a thought. It has been found that speakers who increase volume and the rate of talking are able to gain more attention and interest of others. This knowledge is used by those who produce television commercials. The producers realize that they only have a few brief seconds to display the ads and that they must capture audience attention before they change stations or leave the TV for a break. By increasing the volume and the rate of speech, producers can persuade many viewers to remain and watch the commercial.

Studies have indicated that those who listen to speakers tend to think that those who talk fast are more persuasive and have higher credibility than those who speak below normal speeds. When compared with the average speaking rate of 130 to 150 words a minute, commercials speed up the talking some 25%. Most listeners would prefer a faster speaking rate because the mind is able to process words faster than the average rate, and the faster speakers are perceived as being more interesting. Obviously, school principals cannot be concerned with the rate of speed that they use in talking to others unless it happens to fall regularly below the normal rate. There are times, though, when a more rapid speech and slightly higher volume will enhance a presentation and make the delivery more effective.

Varying the pitch, volume and speed of the voice can be useful, depending upon the situation and the individuals involved. Successful school leaders tend to always be in control of their voice volume and speed when dealing with large audiences or small groups. Dropping the volume and speaking slowly has a calming effect on others and places the principal in an attitude and emotion controlling posture. This approach is useful when dealing with highly upset parents or disturbed youth. If the principal is aware of the other person's emotional state and can control his/her own emotions, it will be possible to defuse most volatile situations.

BODY MOVEMENT

It has been said that "you can't judge a book by its cover." This may be true, but bookstore dealers are well aware that the cover displays on books help to inspire potential buyers to look inside. This is true also of body movement. We are attracted to people that present an overall good impression. These impressions come from appearance, vocal style, and other body movements.

APPEARANCE

In terms of initial contact and impression, the dress and neatness of an individual stands out as a lasting information source. A wise principal who was well versed in job hunting and employment once said, "Dress is one thing that you can control in the interview. Don't blow that part, or for sure you will never get past the other hurdles." Parents, teachers and students expect principals to look their best, and that should remain the standard—look your best! Clothes that make you feel comfortable and relaxed may not be appropriate for all school situations. Teachers, as well as principals, have found that dressing in appropriate clothing and being well-groomed is more helpful in maintaining classroom and school control than being dressed overly casual. Appearance helps others feel that the individual is credible and capable. Most of us expect the doctor to look professional, the lawyer to be well-dressed, and the city police captain to be in a clean and pressed uniform. The same attention to dress is also expected of the school principal who represents the school district.

FACIAL EXPRESSIONS

The face provides the best source of information about an individual's feeling or mood. Facial expressions are often so descriptive that others might comment, "His face read like a book," or "Her attitude was written all over her face." I was in a department store recently on a shopping trip with my wife. As I was sitting by the women's dressing room waiting for my wife to try on a few outfits, I noticed a woman and her teenage daughter in animated conversation. The mother wanted her daughter to try on a particular pair of slacks. The girl didn't want to, and her face was ablaze with anger. "Don't look at me like that," her mother warned. "Then don't make me try that on," the daughter retorted and turned away. The mother's face turned red and she said something that I couldn't hear and probably didn't want to. The old adage, "If looks could kill" came to mind. Ruben (1992) suggests that our faces are capable of creating 250,000 expressions. Fortunately, just a few of the most common expressions provide more than enough information to the typical viewer. Even small children playing make-believe games can mimic expressions of happiness, surprise, pleasure, fear, anger, contempt, sadness and uncertainty. These emotions, in a like manner, can easily be detected in others and provide the observer with valuable information about the speaker.

The face is the best mapped area of nonverbal communication and the place that most of us look to interpret meaning and content. To illustrate your ability to quickly determine the mood and attitude of others, check the meaning that you give to each of the following simple facial expressions. You will probably get at least six of the eight figures correct because they are expressions that are often observed in others. If you miss more than two of the expressions exhibited, you may need to spend more time observing facial expressions as individuals speak to you.

FIGURE 3.1

Match the face with the expression.

A  1. I did it all by myself

B.  2. That's a great joke to play on him.

C.  3. This is a great day!

D.  4. His attitude makes me angry.

E.  5. I really feel badly about that.

F.  6. Golly, did that really happen?

G.  7. I'm sorry to have caused the problem.

H.  8. That decision wasn't fair.

Key:

A—3	**D—6**	**G—7**
B—5	**E—8**	**H—1**
C—4	**F—2**	

What clues did you use to arrive at the meanings of the facial expressions? Now imagine that each of these faces has just responded to you by saying, "Thanks a lot!" Is there a difference when A says it than when C or E says it? At times, facial expressions are attached to an event or occurrence in order to visually express an emotion or feeling. If someone tells us of a death in the family or of an award achieved, that individual expects our face to reflect a personal feeling about the situation. On occasion, it is very difficult to keep facial expressions in harmony with actions and spoken words. Suppose that you observe a student slipping on a banana peel in the cafeteria, and you are reminded of a similar funny incident in a movie. The student performs contortions trying to keep balanced, but lands on his seat with school lunch flying everywhere. You rush over to provide assistance and remark, "Are you okay?" But are you working hard to suppress a chuckle? If so, your reaction may be referred to as a "double communication bind." This means that your verbal behavior follows one path, but your nonverbal wants to go in another direction. Have you ever thought to yourself, "I would like to tell this person what I really think," but instead you say something that is very polite and socially correct, but not at all what you are feeling.

In another case, I can recall as a principal being very stern with a custodian for having placed five cases of toilet paper in the faculty women's restroom because of the continuous complaints of a particular teacher. This teacher protested weekly of the lack of toilet tissue. I had repeatedly reported this situation to the custodian and requested that he check that restroom daily. In frustration, he had written on each case, in large, bold letters the words "for Mrs. Smith." Mrs. Smith was terribly upset with what she perceived as an insult, and I had to respond to the custodian sternly in her support, but must admit that I was amused at the incident and took considerable pains to not smile in front of the two individuals as we met in my office. Thankfully, the situation was defused as a plan for adequate paper was developed and the two left school that day as friends.

EYE CONTACT

The eyes carry expressions that may vary from a mischievous twinkle to a bored, blank stare. Observing eye contact provides a cue to an individual's interest, concern, respect and politeness. These behaviors are considered as positive or warm in establishing relationships (Close, Wiggins & Itkin, 1995). Other warm behaviors include raising eyebrows, wide open eyes, smiling and nodding head affirmatively. Cool behaviors that produce more negative reactions are staring, frowning, looking away from the speaker, shaking head negatively, pouting, yawning and closing the eyes for a period of time.

Direct face-to-face and eye contact depends, a great deal, upon the attraction that is held for the other individual. We like to interact with those that give us a feeling of acceptance and who are friendly. We tend to avoid eye contact if we have something else to do that is considered more important, if we are not interested in the individual, or if the topic being discussed is uninteresting, threatening or causes us to be uncomfortable. I visually recall taking a school law class from a grand old professor who could frighten even the most learned with his piercing stare. At the beginning of each class period, he would call on a student to answer a law question concerning the lesson. If the student didn't know the answer or hesitated, it was an automatic written assignment on the topic. He would begin the class period by placing both hands on the podium and saying, "Well now," as he searched the room for a victim. Some of the students suggested that if you looked him in the eye he wouldn't call on you, but it never happened. Every eye would drop, even the most prepared, because no one wanted to hear his/her name called. I happened to like this professor, thought that he was a fine teacher and most often knew the answers to his questions, but my anxiety always increased during this activity.

People who drop their eyes when you speak to them may be doing so for a number of reasons. It may be a cultural behavior that requires the individual to drop the eyes to show respect to someone older or with more status. Other reasons might be insecurity, a lack of self confidence or uncertainty.

In general, positive feelings toward an individual, interest in the other person's ideas and comments and a high degree of eye contact go together (Ruben, 1992). Principals who engage in more frequent eye contact will be seen as more friendly, helpful and effective in their work and relationships with others.

GESTURES

Movements of the body, head, arms and hands serve as a complement to language. In western culture it is difficult to talk without using physical actions to emphasize the speaker's intent. People who make frequent use of gestures when communicating are usually perceived as more energetic, enthusiastic and responsive to others.

Greetings and salutations often require the most obvious forms of gestures. The wave of a hand, the smile, the nod of recognition and the handshake are familiar to all of us. Principals are constantly meeting friends, associates and guests during school and at social events. The stronger the relationship through professional association or long friendship, the more that is expected in the greeting. Typically, the individual with less status or position in an organization will extend a greeting more readily to a supervisor than vice versa. Thus, when the superintendent drops by the school, the principal, if seated, will stand, move to the door, welcome the visit, shake hands and seat the superintendent first before sitting down. If the principal visits the superintendent at his office, the CEO will be courteous and offer a chair, but may not feel obliged to stand or move across the room in greeting.

Women executives are often confused whether to offer a handshake, wait until one is extended to them, or just greet a visitor without the handshake. With the number of women now in the work force and in leadership positions, the question of social usage is not as prescribed as it once was. The host or school leader should feel free to use the handshake if it is appropriate and a comfortable gesture. One thought of caution in this regard—a "milk toast" or weak handshake delivers a message to the recipient that is not positive. A firm, but not aggressive, handshake is advisable in most greeting encounters regardless of the gender.

Gestures and body movements should always appear natural and support the speaker's ideas and feelings. Overdone gestures look fine on stage and when used by politicians, but excessive movements otherwise appear contrived and insincere. Two cautions are noteworthy when using gestures in conversation. One is to not rely on one gesture and use it over and over. I knew a principal who used to take his glasses off every time he wanted to make a point and then replace them on his nose when he was finished. This action would occur three or four times within a five minute period. Another principal liked to talk with something in his hand that he would constantly turn with his fingers. Both behaviors were very disturbing and distracted from conversations with the individuals.

Nervous type body movements can also distract from an interaction. Repeated straightening of a tie, blowing the nose, scratching an ear, or playing with change in the pocket, for example, can create interferences with the communication process. The best advice is to act natural, be sincere and attentive and not move the arms or body excessively. If excessive arm movements appear to be a problem, place your hands in a coat or pants pocket or hold them at your side.

SPACE

Humans naturally like to be around others to socialize and to accomplish tasks. But, regardless of the situation, most individuals have well defined ideas as to the personal space that they want. Territoriality seems to be a characteristic very essential to feelings of comfort and to our relations with others around us. From an early age, children like their own space and often, this personal territory extends around play toys, backyards and tree houses. Teenagers want their own room and often feel that the family telephone happens to fall within their territory. Home owners define their living space with fences and hedges and go as far as defending their personal spaces with no trespassing signs, mean looking watch dogs and electronic surveillance cameras.

The office and workplace is also divided into work spaces that reflect the personal territory of the inhabitants. Teachers feel strongly about having their own classrooms and are unhappy when it is necessary to share space with another. Even the school principal must have a larger office because the position requires frequent interactions with others. The status of position and added responsibility allows for the reward of increased personal space area. Because of title, those in higher offices in an organization can more easily intrude or enter the working space of subordinates. It is more difficult for the subordinate to walk into the space of the school leader without first being recognized. Some school principals have made an effort to keep their office doors open to make it easier and more comfortable for a teacher, staff member or student to walk in and visit without formality. The principal, regardless of position, needs to remember to be courteous when entering the personal space of others in the school.

Personal space can center on work location as mentioned above, or it can relate to the "my space" bubble that individuals carry around with them. In a one-on-one conversation, "my space" and "your space" is especially important. When two people interact they tend to each establish a personal distance that is comfortable. This distance will allow for personal eye contact and ease in talking. If one individual invades the other's space by standing or sitting too closely, the one whose space is disrupted becomes uncomfortable and nervous. When this occurs, eye contact is difficult to maintain and the body posture will change in an effort to avoid contact and to gain more distance. If the space invading individual's breath is bad, the situation will almost become unbearable.

A preferred social distance when talking is from three to five feet. At this distance, business can be conducted with both parties at ease. Obviously, a noisy office area or crowded corridor may necessitate a closer social distance in order to be heard and to speak without shouting. It has been observed that when people are in crowded locations, school events, socials, etc., they are willing to contract their social space and still feel comfortable.

In most school settings a normal sound distance of three to five feet is usually acceptable for talking.

TOUCHING

In the past few years, touching others within the school environment has become a tenuous proposition. Teachers, staff and administrators who find it comfortable to use touching behaviors in an effort to convey warmth, appreciation and friendship are concerned that such actions might be interpreted as sexually motivated. The number of child abuse and sexual harassment cases in schools, while not extensive, do give cause for care to be taken.

There is a place for touching and the use of kind and caring words in our schools. These kinds of behaviors are powerful and meaningful when used appropriately. Many, youth in particular, need support at school, and touching and/or kind words can give reassurance, appreciation and inclusion that may not be offered elsewhere. A teacher recently came to me with a concern about using the word "love" in class. She reported that she had often told her elementary students that she loved their work or loved them because they were such good students, etc. At a workshop she attended, the participants were advised by an outside consultant not to use the word love when addressing children, as it might send the wrong message. This is a disturbing idea that sincere words of endearment and affection by a teacher might be considered harmful to elementary age children. Teachers are effective because they build self-concept and worth as well as teach subject content. I believe that teachers need to continuously use behaviors that, as William Purkey (1984) stresses, make children feel invited in school.

I recall a tender and touching teaching moment that occurred in an elementary school in Orem, Utah. The time was 2:30 p.m. and school was out for the kindergarten children. I was walking down the hallway and happened to look in one of the classrooms. The teacher was sitting by the side of her desk and had her five year old students in a line in front of her. As a child would walk up to her, she would put her arms around the individual, lift the child up four or five inches and tenderly give a big hug. While she was doing this, she would call the student by name and say, "I like you. You are such a good student, and I love being your teacher." I was so touched by this expression of warmth and affection that I remained outside until she finished and then told her how impressed I was with the individual attention and affection that she gave to each child.

She smiled and told me that she wanted all of her children to leave school each day feeling valuable and appreciated. She then laughingly recounted an incident that had just occurred a few days before. She was in her classroom after school was over checking student papers, when a mother and father walked in with their kindergarten child. "Oh, thank heaven you are here," the mother said with a relieved sigh. "Billie came running home from school and then remembered that he had not received his squeeze from you. He was so upset that my husband and I decided that we had better bring him back to school, hoping that you would still be here." Billie ran to the teacher and got his squeeze and words of praise and left smiling. Later, I thought about how the teacher had touched more than a child. A mother and father had also been touched by the importance of schooling and the worth of a caring teacher.

Touching behaviors should be used to show support and caring to others. These gestures should be kept at a minimum, be equally given to all class members, and be appropriate to the situation and setting. Depending upon the age, gender and grade of the individual, appropriate touching might include a hug, handshake, hand on the arm, or a pat on the shoulder or back. The school principal needs to be reminded too, that adults appreciate a warm handshake, a pat on the back or a positive comment on occasion. This action is great for teacher morale and lets others know that the principal personally appreciates their role and effort in the school.

PHYSICAL ENVIRONMENT

The physical environment includes the entire school facility, but a large portion of a principal's communication occurs in the office. This setting, with its furniture, color scheme and desk arrangement, may facilitate or inhibit information flow.

The office desk usually determines the location of the administrator in the office. The location of the principal has a definite influence on verbal communication. Principals located behind desks and facing visitors from a distance of 7 to 15 feet are perceived as not as friendly and open as principals who use a more informal seating arrangement. A number of principals have moved their desks to the side of the office area so as to create an open and more barrier free setting. When someone enters, the principal has only to turn to the side and he or she will be face-to-face with the visitor. In larger office areas, principals are creating informal discussion areas. These settings include a couch, easy chairs and a lamp and coffee table. The principal also sits in this arrangement, creating a more informal and friendly atmosphere for discussion.

In an interesting study by Lipham and Francke (1966), they found significant differences in the behavior of promotable and nonpromotable principals in structuring their office environment. The promotable principals would move from behind their desks to greet visitors, take coats and hats, and then seat the guests alongside the desk, rather than in front. The distance from principal to guest would normally only be from three to four feet, allowing for an easy and comfortable interchange. The nonpromotable principals tended to seat visitors across the desk with distances being from 5 to 12 feet from principal to visitor.

The promotable principals also liked offices to display their personal tastes and preferences. In their offices, photographs, paintings, assorted knickknacks, awards and graduate certificates would be found in abundance. The opposite was true of nonpromotable principals.

Because many school districts have limited budgets for administrator furniture, some principals have paid for their own office improvements. In one instance, a new principal was assigned to an older school building as her first principalship. She was dismayed at the dull color of the four walls in her office. She had been told by the district that she could request to have the office painted if she desired. The principal requested the money and, instead of the paint, purchased wall paper. She and her husband spent the weekend putting up the wall paper, new drapes and purchasing wall paintings to match the revised decor.

She reported to her husband, "This is more like me." The room reflects her tastes for the area in which she spends much of her daily work time. The office is also more friendly, warm and inviting to those who visit and meet with the principal.

NONVERBAL CUES

Principals should always use nonverbal cues to reinforce verbal communication. The principal, as a listener, can also learn to determine the attitudes and feelings of others by observing behavioral cues. The list that follows includes helpful hints for improving the use of nonverbal behavior:

- As you listen to what someone is saying, be sensitive to the messages communicated by gestures.
- Learn to recognize gestures used by individuals on a repetitive basis. Such feedback will inform you of their personality types and the behavior that they use in an attempt to have needs met.
- Be sensitive to the personal space that others need. Angry or emotionally upset individuals will usually need more space than usual.
- Realize that every move that you make in terms of nonverbal behavior will be observed and inferences drawn about what you're thinking or expressing.
- Use nonverbal behaviors to emphasize, complement, regulate discussion and behavior, and substitute for verbal messages. Attempt to make sure that your messages are interpreted correctly.
- Recognize that touching is a personal behavior and your role as a principal gives you some privileges that should be used with care. Each individual has a touch-avoidance tendency or preference, and this preference can be observed by the characteristics displayed by others during interaction. If touch is not appropriate for some people, words of encouragement or praise may serve as substitutes.

- Use touch behaviors when you want to be positive with another person and you know that they will respond positively to a handshake, touch on the arm or a pat on the back.

Finally, it would be impossible for me to end this chapter without making reference to one form of personal behavior that seems to stand above the others in its ability to affect individuals and influence behavior. The smile is a universal language and communicates a world of positive feelings from the newborn babe to the elderly in nursing homes. I fondly recall a verse by the poetess Emily Dickinson who wrote:

> "They might not need me; but they might,
> I'll let my head be just in sight;
> A smile as small as mine might be
> Precisely their necessity."

A smile always seems to lift communication to a higher level of understanding. People who smile often exhibit behaviors that tend to express sensitivity to others and promote a positive and caring climate. A few years back, my last child, a young son, entered kindergarten. He was so excited to attend, as he had four older brothers and a sister who talked school incessantly while at home.

My wife, son and I met the teacher who was just beginning her career at a pre-school student assessment meeting, and she seemed to be pleasant, but somewhat serious and quiet. As some fathers do, I became involved in my own school responsibilities and didn't spend enough time with my son asking him about his school. I should have noticed sooner that he wasn't behaving like the typical kindergartner who loves the teacher and is excited to run home and present a second by second run down of all the exciting day's news and events at school.

About six weeks after school had started, I casually asked my son how school was going. He just as casually remarked, "Okay." "Okay!" I responded, "Is that all you can say about kindergarten?" We sat and talked for 30 minutes. I asked some exploratory questions, attempting to understand why a five-year-old would only think kindergarten to be merely okay. My grilling went something like this:

"Are you doing okay in school?"

"Yes, dad."

"Are you in trouble?"

"No, dad."

"Does your teacher have to tell you to be quiet or sit still or behave?"

"No, dad."

"Do you like the other kids in class?"

"Yes, dad."

"Then why aren't you excited about school?"

The young five-year-old paused, thought a second, and said, "My teacher doesn't like me." The comment hit me like a sledgehammer. This was a serious statement coming from a little kid who should be thinking that his teacher was the greatest.

"Why doesn't your teacher like you?" I asked quizzically.

He looked at me with his brown eyes and stated without hesitation, "She never smiles at me." My thoughts raced back to the earlier pre-school meeting with the teacher, and I could remember that she hadn't smiled once during the entire session. I supposed that she was new and nervous, and in that situation smiles may not come easily. However, a kindergarten teacher that doesn't smile is in the wrong profession. Imagine my relief when a note came home from the principal's office within the month that the teacher was getting married and would be leaving at midterm to live in another state. I have always wondered if my relief at this move was shared by other parents. I also hoped that her husband would receive enough smiles too.

Why do we like people who smile? Mostly because happy people establish a feeling of personal contact and interest in us. A smile gives a signal that:

- We are reacting positively to another individual.
- We are interested in giving or listening to some message.
- We want to be involved or included with the group to which we are meeting or speaking.
- We want to dispel any tension or conflict that may exist.

SUMMARY

Nonverbal cues not only support the words that we speak, but also contain messages that influence the perceptions and feelings of others. A smile is the most commonly used nonverbal behavior and is considered a positive gesture. However, the behavior is not effective if the principal does not interact with as many of the staff members as possible on a frequent basis. Principals need to be aware that body movements and behavior such as appearance, facial expressions, eye contact and gestures all have meaning and can enhance or detract from a message or interaction.

REDUCING COMMUNICATION BREAKDOWN

Don't get caught in a communication breakdown or blackout. A few simple habits will keep your school on track.

- Treat every person that you meet with a positive attitude. Always be honest and straightforward but also empathetic.
- Whenever you are in doubt about how well a message was received by an individual, immediately go to that person and in a face-to-face setting make sure that you clarify your point of view or the intent of the message.
- If you are concerned about how to best deliver a message, stop before you communicate! Ask yourself, what do I want to accomplish by this message? Will anyone be offended? Am I being sincere and straightforward? At times, it may be wise to ask someone else for their advice on how best to send a particular message.
- Don't send messages or communicate to others when you are angry, hostile or feel out of control. As the principal you must be totally sensitive to

the setting that you are in and how your comments will affect others.

- Don't expect that a message sent is always a message received. Follow up on your communication by being open to feedback and responses from others. If you discover that your message has been received inaccurately, try sending the message again. You should always be receptive to feedback so that you can take appropriate action, if necessary, to strengthen the communication.

BIBLIOGRAPHY

Close, G., Wiggins, N., and Itkin, S. (1975). "Judging Attraction from Nonverbal Behavior: The Gain Phenomenon," *Journal of Consulting and Clinical Psychology, 43*, pp. 491–497.

Ekman, P., and Friesen, W. (1972). "Hand Movements." *Journal of Communication, 22*, pp. 353–374.

Lipham, J., & Francke, D. (1966). Nonverbal Behavior of Administrators. *Educational Administration Quarterly, 2*, pp. 101–109.

Purkey, W., & Novail, J. (1984). *Inviting School Success: A Self Concept Approach to Teaching and Learning.* 2nd ed., Belmont, CA: Wadsworth Publishing Co., p. 8.

Ruben, B. (1992). *Communication & Human Behavior.* 3rd ed. Englewood Cliffs, NJ: Prentice Hall, Inc., p. 210.

4

Listening to Others

A wise man will hear and will increase learning.
—Proverbs 1:5

One way that principals can show support to others is by active listening. Being active suggests that you are being attentive and are in tune with what the other person is saying and doing. By listening carefully, observing physical messages and responding at the appropriate times, it is possible to improve relationships with others and to gain valuable information.

Poor listening always sticks out like a sore thumb. Sometime back, my wife and I were at a formal social event on campus at the university. I introduced my wife to a faculty acquaintance from another department in the college. The faculty member was a gracious individual and immediately began a conversation. I left the two of them for a minute to respond to a request for assistance and later asked my spouse how the conversation had gone. She remarked, "The professor is a very nice woman, but she has a bad habit. As I spoke to her she would constantly glance around the room to see what was going on. On a couple of occasions, she waved to others passing by and I could tell that she wasn't really listening to me. Actually, I wasn't very impressed with her." I am sure that the faculty member didn't mean to appear rude, but her listening behavior wasn't appropriate for the situation and was readily noticed. Once an impression is made about an individual it becomes difficult to change that feeling when encounters occur in the future.

Listening is selective and as a result is difficult to control. We listen and attend to individuals and things making noise to which we attach importance, and ignore or give inadequate attention to those people, events or happenings that are not considered as important. At times scattered listening cannot be helped and may be necessary. School personnel, for instance, are so tuned into hearing and interpreting incoming noises that it becomes second nature to handle a number of happenings almost simultaneously. As an example, I was talking to a principal some time ago while he was on duty at the school cafeteria during the lunch hour. He had warned me that he might be distracted during our conversation. He was! He heard a vending machine being kicked by a girl upset that she didn't receive her change, stopped a boy who was tapping a tune on glasses of water, and upon hearing a food tray being dropped, excused himself in order to supervise picking up the spilled food. Even though he was listening to me, his ears were also tuned to sounds that might indicate disturbances nearby. These types of interruptions are accepted because of the nature of the setting.

When it is important enough to speak to another individual and the setting is appropriate, we generally feel that the person we are talking to should give us full attention. When that does not occur the speaker feels slighted and unappreciated. Actually, listening is a way of saying that I care and that I am personally interested in you and your ideas and feelings. Consider how you feel when someone that you are talking to does the following:

- Interrupts and inserts his/her point of view before you have completed your thought.
- Smiles and waves to others passing in the hallway.
- Nods and closes eyes momentarily, as if fighting sleep.
- Cleans fingernails or looks at watch frequently.
- Says, "Well I appreciate your thoughts on that, lets talk about this later," and then walks away.
- Stares with a blank look somewhere in space and says nonintelligent things such as "ah," "hum," or "interesting."
- Scans notes on the desk while you are speaking.

In each of the illustrations above, the listener is displaying poor manners by not giving full attention to the speaker. Communication is effective when the listener hears what the sender intended and relays that knowledge back with a display of interest.

Have you ever thought about the manner in which radio talk show personalities treat their callers? They invite the radio audience to call in with comments and thoughts, but have you noticed how little the callers get to speak? The talk show host spends much more time talking than listening. Too often, capable and persuasive speakers tend to think that they are good communicators because they can expound so readily on many topics. The more they talk, the harder it is for them to listen. In their rush to get their opinions on the table, they inadvertently become unresponsive to others.

School administrators, by the very nature of their roles as appointed leaders, are busy and have a limited time to spend with the many interactions that they encounter each day. It isn't always easy to devote full attention to each parent, teacher, student and individual who needs assistance or has something to say. These individuals like to be heard, especially by the principal. To attempt to fake listening is as bad as simply ignoring the speaker. When you are rushed for time, you can politely say so to the individuals who ask for your time and give a time frame in which you can communicate with them. Then listen carefully, keeping total eye contact on the speakers. When you must terminate interactions, it is always appropriate to restate the speakers concerns or thoughts, indicate your need to leave, excuse yourself politely and, if necessary, schedule a later meeting.

Listening must rank as one of the school leader's most important communication activities. Yet some studies have indicated that principals talk more than 60% of the time during typical interaction sessions with other individuals.

There are four major activities that the principal must attend to each day. These activities include speaking, listening, writing and reading. More specifically, involvement with others include presenting information and ideas, decision making, clarification of issues, resolving problems, maintaining morale, keeping abreast of educational developments, handling correspondence, etc. The illustration in Figure 4.1 indicates the appropriate amount of time that some educators feel the principal should logically spend on various activities during the school day.

FIGURE 4.1

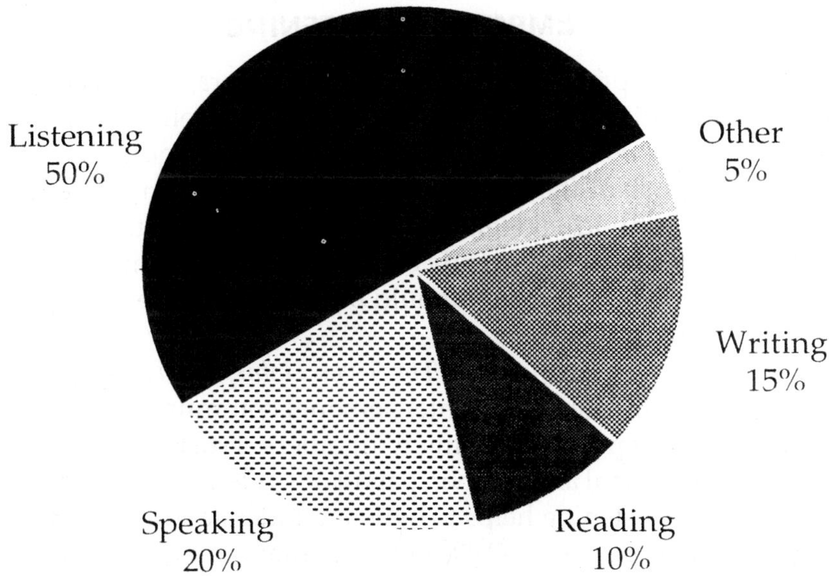

As may be observed, at least one-half of the school day should be spent in listening. Many of us are poor listeners because we feel that we can be more effective when talking. It may not be possible to limit talking time to only 20% of the day, but awareness of how much you do talk and listen will help you to keep a better balance.

Depending on the occasion, listening or speaking may appear to be separate events, but generally the two go together. For example, attending a school play, listening to the choir or band or being a spectator at a sporting event would be considered primarily listening and observing for enjoyment. The only response necessary might be to clap and display appreciation to the directors of the event.

Another type of listening is when attention, as well as an oral response, is expected. At times the school administrator may merely listen to others talk about their problems and then exhibit support and willingness to lend a helping hand if necessary. On other occasions, the support given by the administrator may be to offer directions, advice or suggestions.

EMPATHETIC LISTENING

In order to provide the most help to others, it is necessary to understand what they are thinking and feeling at a very personal level. We may not agree with another's point of view, but it is important that we know what it is and can sense how deeply that individual feels about the issue or situation. It may not be possible to become truly empathic with every individual, but the effort is worthy and should be attempted even if it takes more time than desired.

Steven Covey, in his book *The Seven Habits of Highly Effective People* (1989), indicates that interpersonal communication is the most important part of working with others. Trust and openness between a principal and teacher, parent or student must be earned; and empathic listening helps to build an understanding and sharing relationship. Taylor (1993) reports that empathic listening saves time, improves communication, prevents errors and strengthens morale.

To be empathic requires giving of your valuable time by being attentive to possible problems staff members and students may be having, inquiring if you can be of service and attempting to provide the needed assistance. For instance, even if parents do not know you very well, a phone call, personal visit or card at the time of a serious student illness or some significant student achievement will be highly appreciated and remembered. Likewise, the teacher who is remembered at a critical or important time will be very appreciative and feel accepted as a valuable member of the faculty. Everyone likes to be recognized, understood and appreciated by the administrator who is in charge of the school. This form of interpersonal interaction needs to be a part of the principal's daily organization and shouldn't be expected to occur merely by chance.

I recall an unfortunate incident that happened a number of years ago at a high school in Colorado where I was the principal.

About 9:00 a.m. one of the teachers came to my office with a young student in the ninth grade. He reported that the student had been kicked out of another teacher's class for not having his textbook and swearing at the teacher when he was directed to leave the classroom. As the story unfolded, a classic example of lack of empathy and breakdown in communication had occurred. The boy had walked into his first period class and as he sat down, the teacher questioned him sharply, "Do you have your homework completed?" "No," the boy replied. "Do you have your textbook with you?" the teacher queried. "No!" the boy again reported. "Then get out of my classroom! I told you to come prepared today or not to come to class." As the young student passed the teacher's desk on the way out he muttered to the teacher, "You S.O.B!" The teacher then hotly replied, "That's it! I will take no more from you. Get out! Don't ever come back to this class. You're not welcome."

The boy, in tears, then walked down the hallway to the room where his favorite teacher was holding class and stood in the doorway. This teacher immediately knew that something was wrong and after assigning his class an activity to work on met the student in the hallway. The boy tersely stated that he had been kicked out of class and was running away. The teacher could easily tell by the swollen eye and cut lip on the face of the youth that something traumatic had happened prior to school.

It only took a little encouragement for the youth to tell his story. During breakfast his stepfather had knocked him to the kitchen floor as the result of an argument. The stepfather sat on the boy pinning his arms to his side and then slapped and hit him repeatedly across the face. While he was doing this, he challenged the boy's mother or any of her other younger children to stop him. The family members were too frightened to respond, and the mother would not do anything for fear of her husband's fierce anger. The boy reported that since his mother's remarriage, the physical abuse had been occurring over an extended period of time.

Thirty minutes after this incident the young man came to school, not in the right frame of mind to profit from a first period mathematics class. The teacher had not correctly read the youth's physical signals nor taken the time to understand the poor behavior exhibited by this particular student.

Later, when I mentioned the situation to the first period teacher, he expressed surprise and reported that he had not noticed the facial bruises. He indicated that he would be willing to take the student back in class after I had talked to him about his lack of respect shown to a teacher. The point of this story is to stress the importance of listening and carefully observing the behavior of others, as a means of better understanding feelings and attitudes. The teacher in the first period class had not the vaguest idea of what was going on with this youth, only that he was difficult to work with. Interestingly, the other teacher was considered to be a friend of the student and displayed that relationship by immediately realizing that he was needed and responding accordingly.

The intent of empathic listening is to take the time to listen and to do so with a desire to understand what the other person is saying and feeling. This type of listening requires the use of the ears and the eyes. It is not necessary with this form of listening to sympathize or agree with someone; rather it is an effort to deeply understand that person at an emotional level as well as intellectually (Covey, 1989, p. 241). Empathetic understanding is revealing and therapeutic because it can explain so much as to why others act the way that they do.

LEARNING TO LISTEN

Principals need to actively work and concentrate at becoming effective listeners. Staying with the speaker's thoughts, whether brief or extended, is crucial to good communication. Mind wandering is a problem for all of us unless we are very motivated or focused upon the thoughts of the speaker. The average person speaks around 125 to 150 words a minute, and the mind of the listener can easily record and understand words being spoken at four or five times that speed. While it should be easy, therefore, to record and understand everything that is being said, this is usually not the case. The mind has a very bad tendency to fill think time with other activities. Principals, for instance, can easily review agenda items for the day, remind themselves of appointments, review budget allocations, consider the wording for a parent newsletter item, recall telephone messages that must be returned, etc. Sadly, studies of listening comprehension (Bostrom, 1989) suggests that administrators may only be listening at 25% efficiency. There is a general rule that is a must for good listening to occur. This rule is to simply "stop talking." Reducing the amount of talking time that school administrators think that they need is a challenge, but effective communication involves understanding as well as being understood. To become a better listener, consider utilizing the following as you interact with others:

- Give your full attention to the speaker. Look the speaker in the face as long as you can. If the face you're looking at is not that exciting, focus on nonverbal facial or body physical cues that the individual may be giving.
- Relax your bodily posture, and give the speaker the impression that you are fully prepared to give undivided attention to what is being said. Use eye contact, head nods, smiles, etc., to let the speaker know that you are listening and responding.
- Paraphrase if necessary to make sure that you understand the thoughts of the speaker. To begin a paraphrase you might say, "Let me see if I understand what you're saying. . . ," or "Is this what you meant when you said. . . ?" Paraphrasing provides an opportunity for you to remain in focus with the speaker, to show that you're listening and to avoid misunderstandings if you are not clear about what is being said.
- Listen with a sincere regard and suspend your own views to better hear those of others. A win–win situation occurs when the other individual feels that you have so fully considered his or her viewpoint that he or she simply must, in all fairness, listen to yours.

MARKETING LISTENING

Many school administrators have been in the business a long time. As educators, they know how a school should be run, and they may personally know most of the students in the school as well as their parents. One white-haired and smiley principal from a rural school recently remarked, "I have 500 students in my school, and I can name them all." You know you have been in the school program for a long time when you have taught and worked with your students' parents and grandparents, too." When you live so closely with a job day after day it often becomes difficult to imagine that others might have a different view of the educational process than you have. Times change and people do too. The principal, at any point in his or her career, needs to determine what the customers (all those with a deep interest in education) really think that schooling is doing for the children and what they think of the tax money being expended for education.

Listening should be a scheduled part of the day, just as other events are planned and carried out. Wanting to sincerely listen with an ear toward improving the school and your role as the school leader requires getting up from the desk, putting papers aside and getting out where the action is taking place. This strategy may be referred to as "management by walking around." I call it leadership by intentionally walking around to meet teachers and students, and by listening to their concerns and interests.

One way to be a better listener is "talking to listen." This technique is simply one of making a leading statement that invites the other person to tell you something. Few individuals can ignore or refrain from talking when presented with one of the following statements or questions.

- I am interested in your advice on this situation.
- What would you do if you were involved with this matter?
- How do you feel about the change?
- What happened with the student that you were helping?

- I watched you play at the game on Tuesday; you did really well.
- Can you describe the incident to me?

Always remember to make your statement specific rather than general. For instance, comments such as: "How are you feeling today?" "What's new?" "Have a good weekend!" and "How was school today?" do not invite much of a response and are seen as conversation fillers rather than sincere initiators to engage in meaningful interaction.

Elementary principals often do a better job of visiting classrooms and teachers than secondary principals. High school principals in particular find it difficult to leave the tasks that revolve around the office area. When this is the case, the administrator should make a plan or schedule that permits some time each day for visiting. Teachers and students like to see the principal on their "turf" or territory. Casual contacts make for friendly and relaxed conversations, improved relationships and higher morale among school participants.

Listening times can also be planned as ways to gain information and to make others feel that they are an important part of the school process. People feel and do their best when they think that what they are doing is considered important by others. The following are some good ideas used by school principals to foster interaction, give recognition and improve communication.

- One principal walks into classrooms unannounced and if the timing is appropriate, asks the teachers to call on the students to answer particular questions about the subject areas being studied. When a student answers correctly, he tosses the individual a candy bar from his pocket. The activity only takes a minute, but the teacher is pleased that the principal has stopped by, and the students gain a positive impression of the principal. The cost to the principal is minimal, but the value of the activity is immeasurable.
- Periodically calling 5 to 10 different parents and asking them how they feel school is going for their children. The

secretary or P.T.A. can provide the weekly schedule and phone numbers so that all that is required for the principal is to pick up the phone and talk. A superintendent in Canada did this for a semester with amazing results. He selected a number of at-risk children and parents to contact by phone on a periodic basis. Each home was called at least monthly with an inquiry about the student's progress and an offer to be of any possible assistance. It was found that parental attitudes became more positive and that student performance in school improved.

- Some principals meet with students on a planned schedule in order to improve school relationships. One principal has a system set up in her school where once a week she eats lunch (her treat) with a randomly selected group of students. Her intent is to discover how the students feel about school and to answer any questions they may have.
- A few high schools have vocational food programs that permit parents the opportunity to come to school and eat in a restaurant type atmosphere. Attendance at these dinner times provides the administrator with an opportunity to meet the parents and discuss school events and student activities.
- In Hawaii, the state has funded a "parent in the school" program to improve school and home relationships. The parent works for the year on a part-time basis in the school, helping to improve communication with parents, teachers and the school. School principals are very enthusiastic about the program because of the added help and also because the parents provide useful information about the attitudes of other parents in the community regarding school programs and activities.

THREE REASONS FOR LISTENING

There are basically three types of listening that the principal needs to use in daily activities. These are supportive listening, retention listening and listening to give feedback. Supportive listening is primarily that of indicating support or encouragement to the individual. For example, if a teacher is telling you about an incident at home or in the community that created a problem for them, your task is to listen and provide the type of encouragement or sympathy needed at that time.

Retention listening occurs often when another individual is giving information that you want to remember. Retention is helped if you repeat the key ideas to yourself or if you ask the speaker to clarify the comments being made. There is nothing wrong either in carrying a note pad or record book with you to jot down the ideas so you will not forget the conversation highlights.

The third type of listening is to give feedback. As you are aware, feedback is a form of verbal or nonverbal response to the comments of another individual. Responding is very important because when feedback is expected, accurate listening should have occurred. For example, if in walking down the hallway you are met by one teacher who wants you to check on a book request from a text publisher, another teacher who wants you to talk to a particular student about a tardiness problem and a third teacher who wants to know if he has school lunch duty the next day, these individuals expect that you will remember their requests and will respond appropriately.

With the endless variety of messages being transmitted each day at school, the principal has a constant task of communicating in a timely and accurate manner. One basic communication technique remains constant—that is listening. In many instances, poor communication habits can be traced to a lack of good listening behaviors. As a summary of this chapter, check the listening behaviors that follow and see how effective you are at being attentive to others.

LISTENING SKILLS SURVEY

Listed below are 20 listening behaviors that can add or detract from good communication. In Section I, first column, place a check before those behaviors that you most like to observe in others with whom you are speaking. Then make a check in the second column by those good listening behaviors that you may need to work on to improve your own communication skills.

In Section II, do the same with those items that you feel to be poor listening behaviors. In Section III, list the number that best describes your behavior at this time.

Section I *Good Listening Behaviors*

I like to observe in others: (first column) I need to improve in these areas: (second column)

1. ____ Carefully listens to what is being said. ______
2. ____ Maintains appropriate eye contact. ______
3. ____ Willing to listen until you are finished. ______
4. ____ Attempts to understand your feelings and point of view. ______
5. ____ Does not interrupt to add unrelated comments. ______
6. ____ Paraphrases your comments to gain understanding. ______
7. ____ Nods or moves head and hands to indicate active listening. ______
8. ____ Expresses disagreement without being rude, impatient or disagreeable. ______
9. ____ Seems interested in what is being said. ______
10. ____ Takes the time to make you feel that the message is important. ______

Section II *Poor Listening Behaviors*

I do not like to observe these behaviors in others: (first column) I need to improve in these areas: (second column)

1. ____ Seems in a hurry to be someplace else. ______
2. ____ Does not give full attention and maintain appropriate eye contact. ______
3. ____ Finishes sentences for you as you speak. ______
4. ____ Keeps hands in pockets, plays with keys or other objects. ______

5. ____ Interrupts to add irrelevant comments. ________
6. ____ Dominates the conversation with own ideas. ________
7. ____ Gives negative feedback. ________
8. ____ Seems sleepy or disinterested. ________
9. ____ Works on something else during the interaction. ________
10. ___ Doesn't give positive support to your comments or ideas. ________

Section III

Read each statement and list the most appropriate response that indicates your most common behavior. The scale for each item is: 1) Almost never true of my behavior, 2) Seldom true, 3) Sometimes true, 4) Usually true, 5) Almost always true.

____ 1. I pride myself in being a good listener.

____ 2. I have a tendency to tune out people that I do not like or care for.

____ 3. I enjoy talking and interacting with others.

____ 4. In a typical conversation I will usually speak more than the other person.

____ 5. When I don't understand what another person is saying, I will usually ask for clarification.

____ 6. I am often too busy to listen to others for a long period of time.

____ 7. I seldom lose my composure or raise my voice when speaking to a difficult individual.

____ 8. I usually like to have keys, pencils, glasses or other objects in my hands when I speak.

____ 9. I prefer to listen more than I prefer giving ideas or opinions.

____ 10. I have a problem with being distracted when people talk to me.

____ 11. I usually follow up on requests from others accurately and in a short period of time.

____ 12. I find it easier to listen to certain groups (gender, racial, ethnic, etc.) more than I do others.

Score items 1, 3, 5, 7, 9, and 11 (all odd numbers) as being worth one point for 'almost never true,' two points for 'seldom true,' and so forth. Score the even numbered items exactly the opposite. For example, in statement 2 if you selected 'almost always true,' that score would be worth one point. If you checked that item as 'usually true,' it would be worth two points and so forth. Total the points that you checked for all of the items. If you scored:

50-40: You have very good listening skills

39-30: Places you in the average category with most listeners, but that is not good enough for the type of communication expected of school leaders. If you score in this range, concentrate on improving your weak areas.

29-12: Good listening skills can be learned, and you need to work constantly at this skill to improve your communication with others. Read this chapter again for ideas on how to improve.

SUMMARY

The key to creating good communication is becoming an active listener. Active listening is not an automatic and natural process, especially when strong feelings are evident with an individual or group. However, the principal as an active listener should always do the following:

- Plan time to listen and keep the plan regardless of the situation.
- Always respect the feelings expressed by others.
- Do not interrupt when others are speaking.
- Pay close attention to what is being said.

- Always give an appropriate response that says, "I have been listening."
- Avoid having the final say in the matter.
- Build your comments on the ideas of the other person or group.

BEING A MEMBER OF A SCHOOL OR PARENT COMMITTEE

At times the principal will not be the assigned leader of a group or committee, but will act as a participant. To make the best of these meetings, and not exert undue influence, you should do the following:

- Do not make it difficult for the group leader. Avoid getting into side discussions, speaking too much or interrupting the meeting with an agenda of your own.
- Be supportive of the ideas of others. Do not always feel that you have to be the one to respond to a comment made by a member of the group.
- Pay attention to other speakers. Display interest and enthusiasm for what is happening at the meeting even if you would prefer to be elsewhere.
- Understand your role in the group and act accordingly. Express your support of the leaders and the progress of the group wherever it is appropriate.

BIBLIOGRAPHY

Bostrom, R. (1989). *Listening Behavior: Measurement and Applications*. New York: Gilford Press.

Covey, S. (1989). *The Seven Habits of Highly Effective People*. New York: Simon & Schuster, p. 239.

Taylor, T. (1993). *The Administrators Guide to Personal Productivity with the Time Management Checklist*. Princeton Junction, NJ: Eye on Education, p. 124.

5

SENSITIVE WORDS AND COMMENTS

Colors fade, temples crumble, empires fall, but wise words endure.
—Edward Thorndike

We live in a very sensitive period of time. More than ever, people in organizations want to be thought of and talked to in certain ways that do not discriminate or demean. To some individuals, organizations tend to operate as a system of oppression (Putnam, 1982) in which some members or groups manipulate, abuse, or otherwise subject perceived injustices upon others.

The sources of injustices or undesirable actions that often confront individuals may be in terms of the language that is used and its meaning. In other words, common ways of talking about women or racial or ethnic groups might serve as "put downs," be demeaning and influence ways of thinking and acting toward these groups. Demeaning comments can be sexist language or stories or jokes that portray others in an undesirable condition. At times, sexist comments can also be considered as sexual harassment which includes suggestive requests for favors or physical contact that are unwanted.

School administrators need to be careful as they communicate, to avoid bias or demeaning comments on the basis of gender, racial or ethnic status, age, sexual orientation, or physical or mental disability. Comments that may have been made about these groups in an earlier decade in jest or to tease and were seemingly accepted, will certainly no longer be the case now.

On occasion, a slip of the tongue might occur, and a possible demeaning comment might be made. If an error in speech is suspected, the best thing to do is to apologize immediately and reply, "I didn't mean to say that, and I am sorry if I offended anyone." Unfortunately, a few individuals look to implied negative evaluations of their particular groups and want to feel offended even when innocent mistakes are made. Being aware of possible biases and those who take offense easily, will help avoid falling into difficult situations.

Complaints arise in many organizations that the tremendous emphasis upon correct gender based behavior has created unbearable work relations among men and women. To illustrate I was in a new car agency recently, buying an extra set of car keys. The day happened to be Valentines Day and two bouquets of flowers were sitting on the desks of the two business office clerks who happened to be women. One of the individuals from sales walked by and remarked to the women, "Is it okay for me to say that the flowers are pretty and go well with your clothes, or is that an unwelcome statement?" The older of the women smiled and said, "I will always accept a compliment, thank you." It was obvious that the salesperson, in this instance, a man, was attempting to be careful and not say the wrong thing. He may have known the women well enough, from an extensive period of time working together, that he was certain that the comment would pose no threat to their gender sensitivities. On the other hand, a continuing concern about how a specific situation might affect the sensitivity of another can be confusing and anxiety producing.

For instance, a comment in a similar vein to that described above did not go over as well. A faculty member at a local college entered his department office and, in a happy frame of mind and with a rather loud voice, remarked that the department secretaries (they happened to be women) looked lovely and added a definitely needed, feminine appearance to the office area. His comments, which were accepted by the secretaries as a compliment, were apparently overheard by a woman employee passing the office at the time, and she reported the incident to the dean's office as a sexual harassment occurrence.

In most instances, unless an individual makes a deliberate attempt to harass or demean another person, the party in question will overlook the situation. Actually, such comments or actions can be more embarrassing to the individual making the remarks than the one receiving them. A recent example of this occurred at a gathering of 500 elementary school student body officers for a yearly student council conference. To begin the program, a school administrator (male in this instance) was to introduce the keynote speaker. The keynoter was a well known female television anchor from one of the local network stations. The administrator was obviously nervous and apparently overwhelmed by his assignment. In the introductory remarks, he commented that he was practically speechless by sitting so close to such an attractive and well-known woman. His additional comments continued to relate more to her appearance than her skills as a news reporter. A few of the adult student advisors in the audience were visually uncomfortable and later expressed their discomfort to the program directors. The T.V. anchor was very professional in her demeanor and in her presentation to the audience. She made no reference about the introduction, but went directly to the assignment of talking about student leadership. She was obviously aware that the administrator meant no offense and that her primary task in this assignment was to inspire and motivate young student body leaders in the performance of their school responsibilities.

Few individuals like to be embarrassed in front of others and do not appreciate remarks that are insensitive or detract from their professional responsibilities. There are three questions that an individual should consider when determining if a behavior or comment might be considered as sexual harassment:

- Am I saying or doing something that I wouldn't do if I did not have authority or power over the other person because of my position?
- Is it possible that my behavior will be unwanted or unwelcome?
- Would my behavior be considered sexual or related specifically to the gender of the person with whom I am interacting?

Examples of sexual harassment range in intensity and complexity, but all should be considered when judged on the basis of unwanted or unwelcome sexually related activity. Unwelcome activities may be categorized as threatening, touching or indirect.

Threatening Behaviors:

- Direct or indirect request for unwanted sexual favors.
- Name calling directed at a particular individual.
- Sending letters, notes, or making telephone calls of a sexual nature.
- Stalking or following a particular individual.
- Attempted or actual sexual assault.
- Sending offensive and sexual materials on computers.

Touching Behaviors:

- Patting, pinching, tickling or rubbing against another individual.
- Giving another person a rub or shoulder massage.
- Putting an arm around the other individual's shoulder or waist.

Indirect but Unwelcome Behaviors:

- Sexual jokes or stories that demean the opposite sex.
- Sexual ridicule.
- Bodily motions of a sexual nature.
- Leering or frequent staring at particular parts of the anatomy of another person.
- Sexual innuendoes.
- Spreading rumors about a person's sexuality.

Most principals have been informed by district policy to respond seriously to all complaints regarding sexual harassment. When a complaint is received, the principal will be expected to process harassment complaints by responding to concerns, documenting the incident and following up on the complaint. During the discussion with the individual who has made a complaint, be cautious about making comments that excuse obviously unwelcome behavior. Be careful not to make comments such as:

- I'm sure that he/she was just teasing.
- Oh, he/she puts an arm around everyone.
- We have never had a complaint before—you're the first.
- You're new—just ignore him/her and he/she will stop.
- What do you want me to do?
- Haven't you ever had to cope with this behavior before?
- I can't believe that he/she did that—he/she is always courteous.
- Are you sure that you're not overreacting to a simple compliment?
- He/she probably doesn't mean anything by these actions. He/she is married with three grown children.

These kinds of comments do not help the individual who is upset and is seeking affirmative assistance and support. Be sympathetic, but do not apologize for the individual who has offended. Remember, that you must receive information from both sides and your best professional demeanor will be necessary to help the situation and resolve it to the satisfaction of those involved.

LABELS

Sensitivity to labels must always be considered when talking to others. Do not assume that because an individual or group has acquired a name or label that it is preferred. Preferences will change with time, and "old man," "silver fox," "beauty queen," "babe," "shorty," "tiny," or "Mex," might be descriptive of appearance, but not appreciated. It is usually best to not use a nickname (even if you have heard others use the term) until you ask and determine how the individual wishes to be addressed.

A question often arises as to the most correct way of addressing female teachers or parents. The more polite way is to use the salutation, "Hello ladies," rather than "girls" or "gals." A rule of thumb is to use the terms men and women for individuals over 18 years of age. The terms boys and girls is appropriate for those high school age and under. However, it is appropriate and emphasizes a maturity level to address high school age students by the use of "young man" or "young woman" when possible.

Preferences for names referring to racial and ethnic groups change often due to personal preferences (American Psychological Association, 1994 p. 52). If you are not sure how to refer to an individual's ancestry, it is best to ask about a preferred designation. For example, depending on where a person is from, the preference might be Chicano, Hispanic, Latino or some other designation such as Cuban or Puerto Rican. The same is true of Native American or American Indian for those indigenous to the continent of North America. However, because of the many tribes composing this group (over 400 existing tribal identities), these individuals may wish a particular designation such as Navajo, Hopi, Piute, Seminole or other description.

People of African ancestry also have preferences of relationship to their background. The terms Negro and Colored have become dated and generally not preferred. Appropriate terms today are Black and African American. Of course, everyone is an individual; and using his or her given name will almost always be welcome and appreciated.

A WORD ABOUT WORDS: THOSE THAT ARE NOT GOOD ENOUGH

School leaders need to be able to handle words easily and accurately. Sensitivity to language, both your own, and another person's, can help you to become aware of the differences between words expressed that are most appropriate for the occasion and those that are merely good enough or not good at all. Mark Twain spoke of the use of right words and those that were not good enough as the "differences between the lightning and the lightning bug." A poor choice of words in a particular situation can do the speaker considerable harm in stature, influence and relationship with others. We live in a very sensitive period of time, and cogent thinking is necessary in order to speak well, to influence others and to avoid embarrassing errors that are distracting.

Errors in speaking usually fall under one of these categories: (1) demeaning comments; (2) grammar goofs; (3) gender harassment. Each of these will be discussed in turn.

DEMEANING COMMENTS

To demean another is an attempt to knowingly or even unknowingly, lower that individual's dignity and standing. At times, individuals demean as an effort to encourage someone to do better or to express a disappointment with a particular behavior. While this technique may work well with a few individuals who respond to demeaning statements, most people consider "put downs" to be uninviting, discouraging or antagonizing. For example, review the expressions that follow and consider how often you may hear them expressed at school by teachers, students, staff or administrators. Then ponder how well you consider these types of comments to be accepted by those who receive them.

- You don't belong in this line, get out!
- You speak when I tell you to!
- You can't be that dumb!
- I don't care what you think!
- You're not listening.
- You ought to know better.
- You make me sick.
- That's a childish point of view.
- Sit down and shut up!
- Your excuses are stupid.
- Don't you get tired of griping?
- You are a trouble maker.
- I don't need your opinion.
- I'm in charge here.

Comments like the above are intended to express power over another, are threatening and do not foster harmony and cooperation. There are a number of communication behaviors that encourage others to assume defensive positions within relationships. These behaviors relate to attempts of the speaker to evaluate or judge the behaviors of others, to control or manage other's behaviors, or to make one person superior to the other. Too often demeaning comments have a reverse effect than that intended. The comments may be accepted but the listener will not be impressed or apt to make any permanent changes in the future.

In contrast to evoking negative reactions to comments in an interaction, Gibb (1961) recommends that speakers encourage a supportive climate by describing rather than judging or evaluating other's behaviors, by focusing on specific problems to be solved rather than the individual's weakness, by empathy in looking at things from the other person's viewpoint and by seeing and presenting yourself as equal to others. The comments given earlier that evoke defensive behaviors can be restated to create a more supportive climate and response in an interactive setting. How would you change the five expressions that follow into more supportive statements that do not evaluate, control excessively or display superiority?

Example:

Negative comment: "You don't belong in this area, get out!"
Supportive comment: "This is a quiet zone during lunch. Would you go quickly and quietly to the other end of the hall to talk?"

1. Negative comment: "I'm in charge and don't forget it!"
   Supportive comment: ______________________
2. Negative comment: "Getting three D's on your report card is stupid."
   Supportive comment: ______________________
3. Negative comment: "When I was your age, I showed more respect."
   Supportive comment: ______________________

4. Negative comment: "You don't keep the rules, you get punished and I don't accept excuses."
   Supportive comment: ______________________
5. Negative comment: "Why don't you ever think before you act?"
   Supportive comment: ______________________

Unwelcome comments often have a way of just slipping out of the mouth. These comments may occur when you are tired, hurried or under stress. At times, if we are offended by someone, an immediate reaction is to take the offensive and say something demeaning or negative. The results are generally not favorable for either party. To stop this type of behavior, it is best to follow these guidelines:

- Think before you speak. Ask yourself, "Will my comment add or detract from the discussion?
- Check your demeanor. Individuals who are relaxed and secure do not need to be sarcastic or engage in sharp exchanges. When people are angry or frustrated, they will nearly always match the words that they speak with their facial features and body movements. If you expect an upcoming exchange to be emotional, prepare yourself in advance to be calm, polite and in charge of your behavior.
- Listen before speaking. When you listen to someone, you are creating a positive climate. Actually, good listeners are in control of a conversation because they provide remarks and paraphrase comments of the speaker that cause them to think more carefully of their comments and gain valuable feedback on the mood and motives of the speaker. When the listener begins to understand another person's needs and feelings, it is easier to not be judgmental, defensive or critical.
- Communicate worth. Everyone likes to be accepted and to be appreciated for the role that they play. As a school leader, it is critical that each interaction be a positive one for the participants. When you cheerfully give your time, begin a conversation with positive comments and display

respect for the other individual, the need to speak in a belittling manner will quickly disappear.

REMEMBERING THE GOOD AND THE BAD

Each one of us can vividly recall the kind comments that have been spoken of us over the years. Unfortunately, we also often recall those few unkind words that have come our way for some reason or other. Words have a definite influence upon our lives. A wise thought on communication is found in the Old Testament in Ecclesiastes 3: 1, 7, that indicates the importance that personal comments have upon others. "To everything there is a season, and a time to every purpose under the heaven . . . a time to keep silence, and a time to speak."

Some of the greatest thoughts in the world are those that have personal meaning because they have been directed to us and express a simple but positive and supporting position. Supportive and inviting comments used judiciously and sincerely have amazing results on the behavior and attitudes of others. Following, are 25 of the most welcome and inviting comments that a school administrator can make to others. These expressions are guaranteed to make the recipient's school day and attitude about themselves better.

- Good morning (best used when you also refer to the individual by their first name).
- Hello *(Name)*. Come in and have a seat.
- You did a great job in class today.
- Thank you for the fine job____________ (be specific).
- We missed you.
- You always add so much to our school.
- I'm sending a note to the superintendent about you.
- You are a big help to me.
- Do you have time to tell me about it?
- I would like your opinion.
- I would be happy to write a recommendation for you.
- I have been thinking about you and . . . .

- I received a nice comment about you.
- Can I be of help to you?
- That is a good idea.
- I trust your decision.
- Thanks for following through.
- Thanks for the advice.
- Tell me why you feel that way.
- I really depend on your help.
- Hi (*Name*), how are you today?
- How was the meeting that you attended?
- I'm sorry if I said something that offended you.
- Do you have a minute to help me with a problem?
- Have a good weekend. See you on Monday.

GRAMMAR GOOFS

Administrators talk so much in so many different circumstances, that it is likely that a grammatical mistake in speech will occur on occasion. Infrequent mistakes are quickly forgotten, but English errors that consistently pop up in vocabulary usage jeopardize the administrator's ability to communicate with clarity and confidence. I recall an embarrassing incident that happened to me when I was in my first year as a high school vice-principal in California. The principal and the other vice-principal had been employed in the district for some time and were considerably older than I was. I was very cautious in speaking in administrative meetings because I wanted to express myself correctly. Then it happened! We were discussing the extra factor pay for teachers who supervised at after school events. I reported that according to the records the "renumeration" for such assignments was the same amount as it had been in previous years. The vice principal snorted and laughed out loud, "There is no such word as 'renumeration.'" He chuckled, and his eyes danced merrily at my mistake. Needless to say, I was red-faced, and after the meeting, rushed to my office and the dictionary. To my dismay, I found that the correct word for payment for services rendered was "remuneration." A powerful lesson was learned, and I have used remuneration correctly ever since that incident.

It is not the purpose of.this section to provide a refresher course on the complex rules of grammar or hints for accurate pronunciation of difficult words. It is important, however, that the administrator recognize that speaking errors are common and should be kept to a minimum.

A college type dictionary should be a standard feature on every principal's desk. There are numerous occasions when a dictionary is useful for checking on words that have questionable pronunciations or vague definitions.

There are a few words, common to school settings, which a number of educators mispronounce. Look at the following word lists and circle the pronunciation that you typically use in either column A or B. Check your answers when it is completed. If you miss any, make sure that you correct your word usage so that you won't stumble on these words in the future.

Pronunciation Word List

	A	B
1.	Ek-cet' er-a	Et-cet' er-a
2.	Length	Lenth
3.	Libary	Library
4.	Rec'o-nize	Rec'og-nize
5.	Sim'i-lar	Sim'u-lar
6.	gon-na	going to
7.	let me	lem-me
8.	athalete	athlete
9.	hi-story	hi-stry
10.	gov-a-ment	gov-ern-ment

Correct answers: (1B, 2A, 3B, 4B, 5A, 6B, 7A, 8B, 9A, 10B)

Vocal pauses can also create problems for some individuals. I once had a history professor who had an annoying habit as he paused between sentences. He would stop at a sentence ending and in the process of thinking about the next expression, fill the pause with the vocalization "ah." Actually, he was a knowledgeable teacher and added many interesting insights to his lectures, but his constant use of "ah" detracted considerably from his presentations. Soon, the entire class was counting "ahs," and on his most productive day, he had used the term some 82 times within a two hour class session.

Other awkward and disturbing vocal pauses such as "er," "um," and clearing the throat should be eliminated from speech behavior. If you're not sure whether you use these particular mannerisms, tape a conversation with a spouse or friend for later playback to determine if you use unnecessary vocal pauses in your speech. You may also have an associate listen to your speech in different interaction settings at school to see if you use excessive vocal pauses or particular mannerisms that need to be corrected.

Finally, be aware that the use of the same expression repeatedly to express a feeling or to respond to someone's thoughts may also be considered awkward and unpleasant to others. Expressions such as "you know," "that's great," "well," "really," "etc.," when used without any apparent reference to a comment or idea are merely fillers and mean little to the listener. Recently, I overheard two teachers talking at a social event. They were both agreeing that if their principal told them they were doing a "super job" one more time they would run out of the building screaming. Not knowing how to reward teachers for their support and teaching efforts, this principal thinks that just emphasizing a superlative such as "super job" will be satisfying to teachers. Principals need to remember that what you tell a teacher or any individual is important, but praise and constructive comments must be based upon a relationship that indicates how much you understand the individual, what they do and how much you genuinely care. Repeated comments without specific examples contain little motivation or meaning to the recipient.

EASY GRAMMATICAL MISTAKES

The English language is complicated and the correct use of a particular grammatical rule may be confusing. A careful review of problem areas that you may have will help eliminate the most common grammatical problems. It doesn't hurt to have a concise English grammar and composition book accessible to refresh the memory on items such as when to use "I" and "me," "is" and "are," "was" and "were," "a" and "an," etc. Following is an English grammar quiz to check your use and possible misuse of commonly used words. See how well you do on this test.

English Quiz

Instructions: Read each sentence and circle the correct usage of the pronoun, verb, preposition, etc.

1. She told Helen and (myself, me) about the meeting.
2. I feel (that, like) I should supervise the cafeteria during lunch.
3. The list of individuals receiving awards (are, is) impressive.
4. Neither of you (are, is) right in this instance.
5. The data displayed at the conference (were, was) accurate.
6. The teacher had (a, an) opportunity to attend the county fair.
7. The football team lost because it played (bad, badly) during the fourth quarter.
8. The superintendent liked the report (that, which) I sent him.
9. Tom couldn't get (use to, used to) the new driver training cars.
10. When someone is upset, (they, he/she) will usually display certain facial features.
11. Throwing the book was the (worse, worst) mistake she made in that class.
12. The chorus (did, done) a fine job Saturday evening.

Correct answers: 1. me, 2. that, 3. is, 4. is, 5. were, 6. an, 7. badly, 8. that, 9. used to, 10. he/she, 11. worst, 12. did.

If you missed more than three, it would be useful to pick up a handy English grammar practice booklet and refresh your memory.

WORDS THAT BRING PEOPLE TOGETHER

Words can create a sense of group belonging or exclusion. Obviously in a group setting, such as the school, utilizing a vocabulary that emphasizes group-specific words rather than terms that suggest differences among individuals and groups is desirable. Individuals who tell others how they accomplished tasks, made achievements and told others what to do often arouse feelings of resentment, especially if the tasks and achievements were a group effort. Good speakers or leaders seldom make statements that emphasize "my" plans, "my" decision, "my" initiative, "my" persistence, or "my" leadership. In a like manner they do not emphasize "I and you," but rather use the "we" pronoun that indicates a shared effort. Other group inclusion words that denote support and minimize differences are "teamwork," "partnership," " shared responsibility," and "working together."

SUMMARY

School leaders should be aware of the personal and social consequences of what they say in everyday conversation and in public speaking. It is not easy to separate yourself from the role and responsibilities of being a principal. In the process of sharing thoughts and feelings, it is essential that school administrators respect and show consideration for those with whom they associate. Because people have different backgrounds, experiences and opinions, being sensitive to these differences is a responsibility that imposes unique obligations. School administrators must show care in avoiding the use of demeaning comments. To some individuals, even a friendly tease or jest can be interpreted as a "put down." Bias or demeaning comments that bring attention to one's gender, race, religious orientation, age, etc., should be avoided.

The final measure of a conversation or public speech is the ability to speak positively, clearly and correctly. As a speaker avoid criticism, highly technical terms and offensive language. Be cautious of grammatical mistakes when speaking. If necessary, practice speaking into a tape recorder, paying attention to unnecessary vocal pauses, pronunciation difficulties and grammar mistakes.

ASSERTIVE COMMUNICATION

At times principals must be direct and assertive as they communicate orally with others. Often this is the only means of handling disruptive individuals or problem situations. Assertive statements, if honest and authentic, encourage opinions and help to establish trust and respect. Assertive principals handle interventions in the following ways:

- They seek win-win situations to problems and complaints through effective communication and understanding.
- They use more neutral, descriptive words in handling problems and conflict situations so as not to anger or turn others off.
- They are respectful of other individuals' experiences and abilities. However, assertive principals are not passive, and they do not back down from people who are manipulative or who seek to communicate from a position of superiority.
- They are able to express themselves openly to others and permit others to, in turn, be open with their comments.
- They use physical posturing which is nonaggressive when talking to others. Such nonverbal cues include casual but definite gestures, relaxed facial features, genuine smiles and a firm but pleasant voice that maintains a level tone.

BIBLIOGRAPHY

American Psychological Association, Publication Manual. 3rd ed. (1994). Washington DC: Lancaster Press, Inc.

Gibb. (1961). "Defensive Communication." *Journal of Communication*, Vol. 2., pp. 141–148.

Putnam, L., "Paradigms for Organizational Communication Research: An Overview and Synthesis." *Western Journal of Speech Communication*, 46, 1982, pp. 192–206.

6

Working and Communicating with Groups

It is one of the most beautiful compensations of this life, that no man can sincerely help another without helping himself.
—Samuel Smiles

Interacting in a group setting is central to the functioning of the school principal. Although the school leader will communicate frequently at the one-on-one level to resolve personal problems and facilitate individual goals and expectations, it is at the group level that school organizational needs are met. Much of the problem solving, discussion making, communication within and between groups, day-to-day work and social activity of the school occurs from the functioning of groups (Daniels & Spiker, 1991).

These groups, be they composed of faculty, students, parents, peers or combinations of individuals from various organizations, play a part in gathering information and recommending directions and solutions that directly affect a school's mission and welfare. Membership in a group may be a result of a formal or informal arrangement. Formal groups may exist because of particular functions, responsibilities and established guidelines. The school parent/teacher organizations, PTA, student council, local teachers organization, state associations (with local membership), principals association and subject matter departments in the school are examples of formal groups.

THE PRINCIPAL'S ROLE IN A GROUP

The principal typically has more responsibility and involvement with the structuring and goals of informal groups. These groups develop as a result of immediate school needs and interests. Such groups are often called committees, and membership is delegated or approved by the principal. Committees might be organized to make decisions regarding graduation ceremonies, homecoming activities, fundraising campaigns, curriculum development projects, teacher in-service programming, etc. Informal committees tend to have short lived responsibilities due to the nature of the tasks, but may carry on if the assignment involves repetitive planning and decision making during the course of the school year. Study committees assigned to determine if a particular instructional method is better than another or to investigate the possibility of adopting a new reading program, as an example, may operate for a year or two collecting information and reporting to the staff the findings of the group.

The principal will typically find that he or she plays an important role in any formal or informal group setting . The principal's membership and attendance is critical because of the assignment as leader of the school and as the primary decision maker. Although the principal may not function in a particular group as the assigned chair, the ability of the principal to support group functions and provide necessary rewards and recognition for the participants will help keep the group on task and satisfied with the time and effort being expended. The principal needs to bring to a group at least four special skills (Mintzberg, 1980). According to Mintzberg, the leader needs: (1) peer skills—the ability to keep the group members working together in a positive manner and to reinforce group membership through recognition; (2) conflict resolution skills—the ability to mediate individual and group conflicts and feelings of others; (3) information procuring skills—the ability to network among the members and provide the right information when needed to the appropriate people; (4) decision making under ambiguity skills—the ability to make necessary decisions in unstructured situations under conditions of risk.

Committee or group work assignments generally fall outside of a teacher's, student's or parent's normal work day. In essence, these individuals are volunteers, and they will work more co-operatively and willingly if the tasks assigned are meaningful. Group participation and productivity in meetings will be higher if the principal considers each individual's personal needs and respects the time restraints that are a part of normal life. The principal should be specific with group members in covering such things as task expectations, committee objectives, time tables for completion of events, benefits to the school and students and the need for positive working relationships.

The most effective management of group work on a task is for the principal to be involved as much as possible. Group members often consider the worth of a committee assignment based upon the interest of the principal, his or her attendance at the working sessions, and the quality of oral communication given to this group. The most productive committees make decisions and achieve positive results because of healthy relationships with each other. The school leader plays the role of the team captain, who may not be the most important member of the group, but who fosters an environment that encourages high quality group relationships, and understanding of the talents of each individual in the decision making process.

THE WORKING COMMITTEE

Individuals that come together to work on a task have usually made a commitment to the principal to participate. Agreeing to serve on a committee, however, doesn't necessarily imply that the individual is totally prepared to meet the principal's or the group's expectations. There is a human side to group work, and participants come to a meeting with differing expectations, agendas, attitudes, interests, and motivations.

The principal needs to be aware that groups form an identity similar to that of individuals. With time, a group will develop its own set of practices, values, norms and social relations. On occasion, this polarization will cause some members to want to withdraw from the group because they feel pressured to accept group norms. Other members will learn to give, take, resolve conflicts and make accommodations among members in order to insure progress toward completion of the task. Ruben (1992) indicates that through verbal and nonverbal behavior, individuals in a group create a culture, symbols, rules, and even jargon to express the culture of the members. Once created, the culture of the group "acts back upon" its members to influence participation and reliance upon rules and expectations.

Individuals may behave differently in groups than they commonly do when they are not in groups. Often quoted is the classic study on group roles by Benne and Shents (1948) that is still accepted today. The authors outline three types of roles that individuals will assume in a group over a period of time. These are: (1) completion roles such as information/seeker, elaborator, coordinator, evaluator/critic, procedural-technician, recorder, etc.; (2) group building and maintenance roles such as encourager, compromiser, standard setter, group observer, and follower, etc.; and (3) individualistic roles such as aggressor, blocker, recognition seeker, dominator, and deserter, etc.

Benne and Shents do not suggest that every given member of a group plays only one of the roles. At times, a member will change roles depending upon the situations and group membership, but some roles seem to fit the personalities of individuals. In many instances, the caregiver type who encourages others and attempts to reduce conflicts among members tends to always assume that role. On the other hand, an aggressor may shift or blend with the blocker, recognition seeker, or dominator roles, but seldom with follower or harmonizer group functions. Observing the roles that members play in a group and understanding that such behaviors are to be expected, can help the principal in keeping the group focused upon its responsibilities.

Within this setting, the role of the principal becomes complex. The luxury of assuming one of the three types of roles as mentioned above, may not be to the best benefit of the group. In a small working group, the principal's role may be subtle, but encouraging. Membership in a larger group may involve stronger and more noticeable leadership, but not domination. The leader should serve as a coordinator, assisting individuals to express themselves, encouraging group building and support, providing necessary information and a vitality that will contribute to the group's success. Devito (1988) recommends that leaders in a group carry out six major functions in order to keep the work productive. These functions are:

- Activate group interaction. Encourage interaction and build group task responsibility.
- Maintain effective interaction. Do not let meetings drag. Make sure that some members do not dominate group time and that the others have an opportunity to express themselves.
- Keep members on task. Ask relevant questions. Make sure that an agenda is prepared and followed. Don't let discussion wander off of the topic.
- Ensure member satisfaction. Give praise when needed and earned, and be responsive to individual needs and attitudes. Support digressions as long as they do not detract from group members and task goals.
- Encourage ongoing evaluation and improvement. Assist the group in overcoming obstacles and frustrations as they attempt to solve problems, reach a decision or develop ideas. Have the group recap the progress made at the end of each meeting and also point out areas that need improvement. Do not let the participants become too discouraged if progress seems overly slow. Help the group visualize problem areas and discuss how they can be resolved.
- Prepare members for the discussion. Keep meetings organized and friendly. The leader needs to prepare the group for the meeting by including a warmup activity or discussion. The agenda and items of information need to be prepared in advance of the meetings and revised as appropriate.

The principal needs to reward group members as goals are achieved. When members of a group are upset, it tends to affect the entire group negatively; when all are happy, the group tends to polarize and maintain task responsibilities.

CONFLICT IN GROUPS

Conflict seems to be inevitable in groups, especially when the participants have not worked closely together on other occasions. Conflicts may arise over individual expectations for the group's goals, member roles and responsibilities, group dynamics, individual sensitivities toward certain issues, or any number of factors. Conflict is often a natural part of the exchange of ideas, and indicates that the group members are interested in the topic, have suggestions for problem resolution or can visualize an alternative point of view. The principal can reduce conflict by understanding why conflict occurs and how certain individual styles and mannerisms can create feelings of harmony or unrest among group members. While some conflict is natural, attacks on personalities should be avoided. Serious problems can arise in the functioning of a group when a conflict centers upon individuals and not issues. When these problems occur, the principal may wish to instruct the group to center its focus upon issues by considering these basic rules of behavior for group settings:

- Conflict or disagreement is healthy if confined to issues.
- All points of view should be considered in a discussion.
- When someone disagrees with what you say, do not consider this as a personal attack.
- Do not say to another group member, "I disagree with you," or "You are wrong." Make it clear that your disagreement is with the proposal advanced, the solution offered, or the ideas expressed.
- Accept the contributions of all members and encourage everyone to generate ideas and information, if they feel so inclined. Encourage group and individual support of committee goals by the use of appropriate guiding oral statements. Some examples are given for each of the six major group functions.
- Group work is a shared responsibility and individuals in the group should not satisfy their need for personal satisfaction at the expense of others. Excessive solo performances frustrate and hinder the progress of the group.

At times the principal will need to make specific comments to maintain group cooperation and harmony. Some possible comments for various group situations are listed below.

- Encourage Group Interaction:
  "What tasks do we need to accomplish at this meeting?"
  "Who will be responsible for this assignment?"
  "Do you have any idea how we can accomplish this goal?"
  "What do you think about this plan?"
- Maintain Effective Interaction:
  "Let's make sure that we hear from everyone."
  "We should move to the next item on the agenda."
  "Shall we schedule the meeting time in order to accomplish our tasks?"
- Keep Members on Task:
  "Those are good comments—any more ideas about this subject?"
  "Let's be specific about these points. What do each of you think that we should do?"
  "We should attempt to settle this issue before we move on."
- Ensure Member Satisfaction:
  "That's a good suggestion—what do the rest of you think?"
  "It is obvious that you spent a lot of time on the assignment—thanks for your good work."
  "Thank you for your contribution to the group."
  "We are making good progress—I am pleased that we are meeting our goals."
- Encourage Ongoing Evaluation and Improvement:
  "What have we accomplished to this point?"
  "Let's not worry if it takes longer than we thought to solve this problem."
  "Let's discuss ways that we can solve this problem."
  "How can we determine if our plans or goals are appropriate?"
- Meeting Preparation
  "Let's whip around the group and have each member tell what has happened since our last meeting.

"I have given each of you an agenda—give me your suggestions for any changes.

Ruble and Thomas (1976) stress that conflict results from the assertiveness of some group members and the desire of others to be cooperative. From these two dimensions arise five different styles of conflict that members may assume. These are: (1) Competitive style, in which the individual is very high in assertiveness and low in cooperativeness. (2) Accommodative style, in which the individual is low in assertiveness and high in cooperation. (3) Avoiding style, in which the individual is low in assertiveness and low in cooperation. Examples of this behavior are indifference and group isolation. (4) Collaborative style, in which the individual is high in assertiveness and high in cooperation. (5) Compromising style, in which the individual is moderate in both assertiveness and cooperativeness. In the compromising style, the attitude is to compromise in order to resolve conflict, agree upon decisions and keep the group moving forward.

In addition to resolving conflict that might arise in a group, the principal also has other tasks that require communication skills. Baird and Weinberg (1981) list promoting participation, regulating interactions, promoting need satisfaction, encouraging cooperation, assuming responsibility for group failure, and promoting group development as the most important things that a leader must accomplish in a group. Each of these tasks requires that the principal be adept at oral communication in keeping the group members on task and cooperating with one another.

GETTING THE MOST OUT OF GROUPS

Group work in the school serves an important function in decision making and in developing individual values and attitudes toward the school program. The group effort may be very productive and cooperative or uncertain and plagued with conflict. Conflicts, uncertainty and membership withdrawal can result if the members have no clear sense of the group's mission, the principal's functioning within the group and individual member responsibilities. Other problems arise when the principal or leader dominates the meetings and pushes a personal agenda until it is adopted by the group. Infrequent meetings, poor scheduling and timing for the individuals to get together and spotty attendance by members result in the group's not developing a sense of identity, worth and influence.

GROUPING WITH A PURPOSE

Groups can be organized with specific functions in mind. Depending on the type of interaction that the principal wishes to achieve among group members and the task to be completed, the principal may have a centralized or decentralized grouping. Groups may be structured into one of five most frequently used patterns. The major difference in the group structure is the degree of centralization. Highly centralized structures rely on the leader giving instructions and receiving feedback from each member of the group. (See Fig. 6.1 for examples of each structure. The arrows indicate the typical flow of messages from one individual to another).

FIGURE 6.1

Group Structures and Interaction Patterns

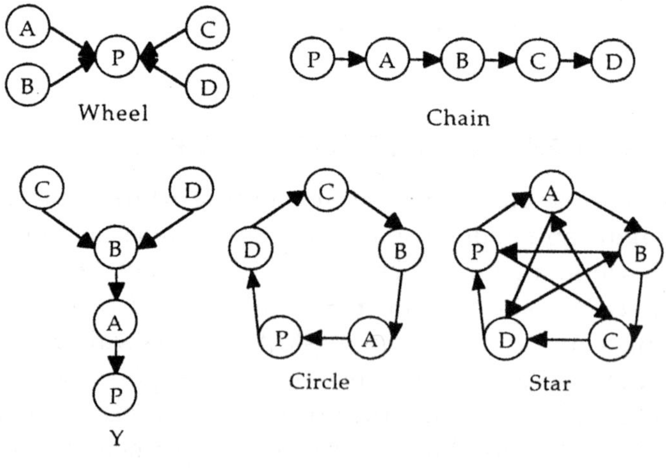

The letter P designates the principal as a participant in the group. The other letters represent other group members.

THE WHEEL

In this grouping, the principal is clearly the leader. For instance, the principal of a large school with three or four vice-principals may assign labor specific tasks to each subordinate. Each vice-principal has a specific task, such as discipline, scheduling, supervision of teacher performance, student activities, etc. The subordinates send information to the principal and the principal sends information back, usually in the form of directions and decisions. This system works well because communication is centralized and communication is kept relatively simply within the confines of a few individuals.

THE CHAIN

Chaining is a communication network that is centralized and often occurs as a result of the existing organizational structure in the school. For instance, the principal may tell a vice-principal to give information to individuals over which he or she has responsibility. A typical chain arrangement would also be one where the principal (A) gives information to the department heads, (B) who report to their teacher, (C) who provide information to their students, (D) who respond back to the teachers, who relay the information back up the chain. Another example of informal chaining is the grapevine through which information of all variety passes from individual to individual between and among different departments and organizational levels.

THE Y

The Y pattern is similar to the Wheel where the principal is clearly the leader and focal point of all communication. This pattern is also a branching organization because the other member nearest to the principal may send and receive information from more than one other individual. However, information that comes through this network will generally always return the way that it was sent. The dynamics of organization today suggest that morale is improved and participation of group members increased when they have been involved in making decisions that affect them. While centralized group arrangements are effective in accomplishing simple communication and organizational tasks, they do not allow for more members to be involved in decision making responsibilities. To increase participation, school leaders may use the Circle, or Star network.

THE CIRCLE

The Circle may have a leader, but the group organization promotes total equality. The principal, in essence, and without fear, gives up authority to permit each member of the group to influence others. Members may communicate with the two members on either side of them as they discuss problems. At times, the group may break into small working committees (usually three individuals) to discuss a problem component and to report back later to the total group. In the circle pattern, everyone can become a decision maker and report to those on either side with equal communication opportunities.

THE STAR

The Star pattern is similar to the Wheel, however, the big difference is that the principal is not the focus of interaction as occurs in the wheel pattern. The star pattern permits each member of the group to communicate openly with all other members. The principal may be a member of the group, but does not assume a dominant position and does not encourage communication to center on his or her position in the group.

Obviously, the results of a decentralized pattern of organization to complete tasks can increase membership morale and personal satisfaction. However, this will ultimately be dependent upon the principal's willingness to support group recommendations. The sensitive responsibility of the school leader in using the Circle or Star group patterns is to encourage member participation, to temper the desire to control or direct suggestions and ideas and to remain involved enough in the task process to predict and support the results.

Principals can avoid the potential problems of using groups by being considerate of individuals' time and energy, by having well thought out, and relevant tasks to perform, and by detailing the responsibilities of the group members. Frequent meetings that are not overly long and have a prepared agenda are appreciated by group members. The first few meetings of the group should permit time for the members to become self-oriented to the other members. This is considered a crucial phase of group membership and determines, to a large degree, later productivity. According to Schein (1948) who analyzed group behavior carefully, it is necessary that group members have time to determine their role and function in a new group. Self insights include personal questions such as: Can I relate to the members? Do I have something to offer? Will this group accept me? Can I exert influence in this group? Does the group's directions, goals and values agree with my own? A member's status in the group depends, to a large degree, upon the quality of interaction patterns with others and the extent to which the individual feels accepted and is respected by group members. The principal needs to be sensitive to the coping behaviors that each group member will place into operation, and provide the time and support for individuals to "fit in" and become comfortable.

The work of the group can provide the administrator with a number of positive approaches for building school morale and productivity. For example:

- The group makes solving school problems manageable. A group can tackle a task and arrive at acceptable solutions much better than the faculty as a whole.
- The principal can place individuals in a committee who represent differing opinions in the school. These individuals may have varying agendas or ideas about what should be done to resolve school problems and how tasks should be accomplished. The group membership over time will often reach a common norm and sense of school values that will frequently negate extreme positions.
- Groups create links among members that strengthen the school through shared information and better understanding of the total school program.

- Group members interact with other faculty and share the work of the group, thus giving all members a feeling of involvement and understanding of the decision making process.
- Groups have a closer contact with the school administrator and feel a stronger sense of involvement in the work of the school.

THE GROUP MENTALITY

For centuries, individuals have come together in groups. All of us like to be with others who seem to be similar in values, attitudes and behaviors. Even in prisons, individuals who have found themselves outside the normal stream of human conduct and socially accepted behavior find acceptance with their cell mates. Each group forms as a result of some need for collective behavior. Religious groups often place the emphasis upon fellowships and striving for salvation in this life; political groups strive for dominance in government in order to keep a philosophical social structure intact; environmental groups express deep concerns for nature and a continuing green and beautiful earth; and work related groups push for authority in order to meet human needs and fair wages and benefits. Inclusion in groups is usually considered a mark of interdependence. Most individuals with any social drive want to be needed. Each of us is a social being, and our institutions are social units that require the work and efforts of individuals. Individuals in group situations have a deep-seated desire to contribute in some way. All groups, to be viable and long living, must include certain characteristics that meet the needs of the participants. These are:

- Sincerity and trust.
- Being needed.
- Being cared about as an individual regardless of background, behavior and physical characteristics.
- Being involved and productive in the group's goals and objectives.

- Having the opportunity, if necessary, to stand up and be counted as a member of the group.

Groups invariably form in school settings as members come together as a means of sharing, increasing personal satisfaction and gaining attention and decision making power. The Parent Teachers Association (PTA), for instance, have had groups of parents involved in school functions for years in order to display parental support for the schools. Some temporary parent groups form, specifically, to increase pressure on the schools for better bussing service, better safety guards at traffic intersections, improved school lunches, etc. Teachers form groups such as the National Education Association (NEA) and the American Federation of Teachers (AFT), in order to obtain better working conditions for their teacher members. These groups establish norms and working relations that members are expected to follow. Dues paid to the organization help publish news reports on the function of the organization, provide insurance against lawsuits, support grievances against unfair administrative practices, etc.

At times, the intensity of member involvement in a group can be disconcerting to the school principal and the morale of the faculty. I recently received a call from a young principal who was undergoing his first teacher dismissal process. In this instance, the teacher has filed a complaint against the principal and school district, and has asked for a board hearing. Two groups were visibly forming in the school—those who support the teacher and her request for reinstatement, and those who support the principal and school district, and do not favor reinstatement. The principal expressed concern about having on hand the necessary evidence to present a complete and rational case for dismissal. He was also concerned that a division in the school among the teachers and students could be lasting and damaging to school morale and well-being. While a teacher group may appear to be homogenous in a number of beliefs and attitudes, teacher dismissal, if full-blown and lengthy, can create opposing, bipolar factions. The best way for a principal to handle such situations is to be ethical in making any comments about a teacher's performance, keep others informed of the dismissal process, let the records (case materials collected) speak for themselves at the proper time, and to not let the problem effect other school interactions and issues. In advance of problems arising over issues of this nature, the channels of communication must be open, and others must be aware that the principal has been committed to doing everything possible to resolve the problems in a concerned and correct manner.

Signs that a particular group is becoming too cohesive, narrow in focus and less apt to work productively with the school goals include these behaviors among members:

- Tendency to see only one point of view
- Increased separation of members from others. The group often sets its own agenda and unwillingly participates in activities planned by others.
- Pressure for others to join the group or to support group goals.
- Competitive style that is becoming combative, including efforts to create conflict over issues that could normally be resolved without difficulty.
- Group members think and behave differently from the way they would act away from the group.

Groups that become too obsessed with a cause often lose the ability to consider the long range effects of their actions. For example, one militant teacher group in a large high school in a western state, upset with the district's proposed salary increase, encouraged students to walk out of school, called the news media about the student walk out (its time and place), held a mass teacher and student meeting at the entrance to the school, wrote "walk out" music and lyrics, and led the singing during the mass meeting.

Whenever possible, the principal needs to diffuse the behavior and actions of groups that lose focus and control. To do so, the principal needs to be "inclusive driven." That is, he/she needs to accept diversity in teacher, parent, and student members; see others' points of view; and be able to express contrary opinions without being rude or disagreeable. Everyone is needed in order to make a school operate successfully. The principal's best tool in keeping others feeling included in the larger group mission is communication and a lot of it. When individuals feel involved and included, they are more apt to be understanding and appreciative of the system in which they work.

Groups are essential and valuable to the operation of the school program. The principal needs to encourage positive group behavior by displaying trust, encouraging responsibility and accountability and providing the opportunities for personal development of individual members.

GENDER DIFFERENCES IN GROUPS

Regardless of gender, individuals will assume certain roles as they come together in group situations. Variety keeps group activities interesting, and the perceptive principal will want to make certain that any working committee has the necessary representation of members whether it be gender, age or task interest. Males and females bring unique characteristics to group meetings, and these talents are needed in order to accomplish group goals in a successful manner. As the gender of individuals in a group may have an impact upon the direction of conversation, the relationship between interactants, and the progress toward developing solutions to tasks, the principal needs to understand the differences that may exist and how these differences may affect group activity.

Task responsibility: Women tend to be just as task oriented as men in assuming responsibility to meet group goals or to complete tasks. During relaxing conversation periods, however, men will often focus upon sports events while women may prefer to discuss clothing, furniture, children and other household responsibilities.

Conversation styles: Women tend to be more responsive to emotional appeals, while men tend to reason more objectively. Recalling information from a message seems to come easier for women than it does for men.

It has been observed that men are more apt to interrupt a conversation than women. Men often are interruptive primarily as a means of controlling content, while women will interrupt usually to express support or to indicate willingness to keep the conversation going.

Vocabulary Usage: Women and men tend to use a larger vocabulary when they are discussing topics of interest. To a large degree, men enjoy talking about sports more than women, and will utilize more readily, the particular slang associated with a sport (i.e., "kill the bum," "rubber arm," "no guts," etc.). Women, typically, are more cautious in using correct English in speaking and usually are more aware of grammatical rules than are men. Contrary to the stereotype (this thinking may have been generated by males), men generally talk more than women. In some studies, men talked four times as much as women. Men, it was found, often use more words per utterance than women, especially if they are responding to negative criticism (Ruben, 1992, p. 364).

There is little truth in this age that leadership skills differ among men and women. Some men will prefer working for male leaders, and others will feel comfortable following the leadership of women. This is true of women also, and while a few will state that they do not like to work for other women, most do not care as long as the manager meets their expectation and provides positive experiences. It has been suggested that today's workers like female leaders if they are effective communicators, and if they serve as mentors and help others. Workers tend to like male leaders if they are effective communicators and assume roles of a friend or buddy. It appears that workers want to be able to get along with their leaders and feel accepted.

Stereotyping of male and female leaders, although changing, will continue to abound for some time. The important thing to remember is that most people enjoy their own gender and want to be accepted for the contributions that they as women and men can make. The principle of fairness should apply to the manner in which men treat women and vice versa. Treat each person as you would want to be treated is still in style. With this attitude, gender differences should have little bearing on treatment in the work place or social gathering.

EVALUATING THE PRINCIPAL AS A GROUP MEMBER

Working in a group can be a challenge to the principal. Depending upon the group make-up and responsibility, the amount of authority the principal should display is not always clear. Should the principal always assume leadership of a group? Should the principal be passive, listen intently, but let the group leadership emerge? Should the principal assume a "hit and run" posture by giving direction and feedback when it appears to be necessary, and then pull back from the group interaction in order to let others participate? Answers to these questions will depend, to a large degree, upon the membership and functions of the group. Good leaders, however, are aware that leadership functions are preferred when they are nonobvious and nondirecting. The more direct and assertive the principal becomes, the more likely that others will lose interest in participating.

Whatever role the principal assumes in a group (assumed leader, or participating member), there are functions that need to be performed to assist the group in achieving its tasks and goals. The form that follows is a useful one for school leaders in evaluating their performance in group situations.

If you were unable to check each of the items in the chart with a "most of the time," or "always" mark, plan on spending more time and effort in this area to improve your participation skills.

Principal Group Member
Evaluation Form

Check the degree of participation that you exhibit in each of the items that follow.

As a school leader I . . .	Always	Most of the time	Some of the time	Little of the time
1. Listen attentively when others are speaking.	☐	☐	☐	☐
2. Express a positive attitude about the responsibilities of the work group.	☐	☐	☐	☐
3. Keep my comments, suggestions and directions at a desirable level of frequency.	☐	☐	☐	☐
4. Recognize the contributions of others.	☐	☐	☐	☐
5. Remain open minded and willing to change ideas or solutions if group ideas are better than mine.	☐	☐	☐	☐
6. Realize when a conflict is personality centered and appropriately redirect the discussion to issues.	☐	☐	☐	☐
7. Explain to the group my role and expectations in the beginning of each session.	☐	☐	☐	☐
8. Recognize the roles played by group members by observing their behavior.	☐	☐	☐	☐
9. Use the information about roles played by group members to keep individuals working cooperatively with others.	☐	☐	☐	☐

If you are currently working with a group of parents, teachers or students, can you place group members in one or more of the role behaviors listed? As you might expect, some individuals play more than one role and can easily be placed in two or more behaviors. Once you have determined the roles played by the individuals in a group, how can you use this information to help you meet group goals and encourage cooperation?

Group Task Roles		*Group Maintenance Roles*	
Recorder	____________	Leader/Task setter	____________
Information and Opinion Giver	____________	Encourager	____________
Contributor	____________	Compromiser	____________
Summarizer	____________	Group Observer	____________
Evaluator	____________	Follower	____________
Coordinator	____________	Praise Giver	____________

Individual Roles Group Goal Distractors

Aggressor ____________

Recognition Seeker ____________

Dominator ____________

Confused ____________

Blocker ____________

Disinterested ____________

Cynical ____________

By observing and being able to place those with whom you work and associate in behavior categories, it will be easier for you to relate to their participation styles and to know what to expect during interaction.

SUMMARY

The purpose of meeting in groups is to organize the members to accomplish organizational tasks. The principal needs to be socially responsible in group settings and give direction, praise and encouragement when it is necessary. The principal is visibly present in every meeting and as the leader must demonstrate awareness of group goals, the feelings of members and the importance of building team success. The most effective meetings are designed to build a sense of support and community among participants.

Building teamwork and cooperation among group members requires the development of a supportive organizational climate. When a group is organized to perform a function or complete a task, the principal should have in mind concrete plans for the group to follow. These plans should include specific objectives to be completed, the function of each committee member, a schedule of activities and deadlines and how the results of the group's effort will be used. Any reward or encouragement that might be given to the group, in terms of time off from classroom assignments to meet, refreshments, gifts of appreciation or a suitable recognition on completion of the project will be positively received by those who participated.

BUILDING GROUP RELATIONSHIPS

Group work is a large part of a school administrator's job. The principal must balance carefully the need to make decisions and to do so quickly with the slower pace, discussion and compromises that must occur when groups work together on a task.

Group members need to trust the school administrator when staff members are asked to give time to serve on a committee. These basic ideas are essential in establishing trust with a group.

- Be sure that what you say about the function and work of the group is accurate to the best of your knowledge.
- Keep the group informed of any changes in assignments or group goals.

- Remember to praise group members in public and to criticize or offer suggestions to individuals in private.
- Follow through on commitments to the group. If you schedule a meeting, make sure that you can attend.
- Do not have your mind made up on suggestions from the group, and be willing to compromise and accept the good ideas of others.
- When things go wrong be willing to accept your share of the disappointment and blame. When things go well spread more credit to the others than to yourself.

BIBLIOGRAPHY

Baird, Jr., J., & Weinberg, S. (1981). *Group Communication*. 2nd ed. Dubuque, IA: Brown Publishing, p. 215.

Benne, K., & Shents, P., "Functional Roles of Group Members." *Journal of Social Issues*, Vol. 4, pp. 41–49.

Daniels, T., & Spiker, B. (1991). *Perspectives on Organizational Communication*. Dubuque, IA: William C. Brown Pub. p. 233.

Devito, J. (1988). *Human Communication: the Basic Course*. New York: Harper and Row, Pub., pp. 266–268.

Mintzberg, H. (1980). *The Nature of Managerial Work*. Englewood Cliffs, NJ: Prentice-Hall, pp. 62.

Ruben, B. (1992). *Communication and Human Behavior*. 3rd ed. Englewood Cliffs, NJ: Prentice-Hall, p. 364.

Ruble, T., & Thomas, K. (1976). "Support for a Two Dimensional Model of Conflict Behavior," *Organizational Behavior and Human Performance*, Vol. 16, pp. 143–155.

Schein, E. (1969). *Process Consultations: Its Role in Organization Development*. Reading, MA: Addison-Wesley Publishing.

7

Communication With Difficult People

Always do right. That will gratify some people and astonish the rest.
—Mark Twain

Don't waste your time in carping, disliking, griping, envying, resenting, hating, hurting. All the dividends you receive will be to get it all back in kind . . . so there is no gain. However, if you return love for hate, it will be the right thing to do and besides, it will make your critic feel cheap. *—Edgar Dale*

Any time two or more people get together there is always a chance that disagreements or differing points of view will occur. Conflict between individuals may be little more than a state of disagreement that is simply resolved and forgotten, or exists at a level of hostility that lasts well beyond the occurrence that created the conflict. Superintendents are fired by their school boards over incidents that occurred months earlier and were not forgotten. At times, individuals run for the school board hoping to be elected so they can get rid of the superintendent or principal with whom they had a disagreement. On occasion even a principal's positive comments to an individual can later be turned into a negative situation. I have heard a teacher remark about her principal, "I will never forgive my principal and never trust her again." When asked why, she said, "Two years ago, the principal said that I had a good chance to become a vice principal in the school district when an opening occurred. She encouraged me to return to school and get my administrative credential. I did, and a job came open. I didn't get it. I don't think that she worked hard enough for me to get the position."

Conflict cannot be avoided, but it can be minimized by understanding that difficulties with individuals and groups often arise because of perceptions that we hold for ourselves and others. We have a tendency to avoid or stay away from those individuals who do not think like we do, or who seem to rub us the wrong way. Our friends and close associates become people with whom we feel at ease and can relate to on most occasions. With friends, communication seems simple because our words and actions meet each other's level of acceptance and expectation.

Most organizational goals and functions cause individuals to come in contact with one another. Teachers in the school building must work with the students assigned to them, and principals must provide leadership to the teachers in the school, the students and the parents. The school principal, as the appointed leader, seeks unity of purpose and team work to get the job done to everyone's satisfaction. It might be easier to accomplish the purposes in mind, if all associates are friends or have similar thoughts. But as everyone who has experienced some form of corporate or socialized life knows, it is not always possible to associate only with friends or "think alikes." Work assignments often place individuals in close relationships in which there is no chance but to interact. They must get along or all types of negative results will occur.

In numerous school settings, I have heard some teachers remark about their class of students, "If I could only get rid of four or five students (about 20% of the students in the class), I would have a wonderful teaching experience." Principals have remarked in a similar fashion, "About 20% of my teachers make my work difficult by constantly creating problems." It may well be that school superintendents say the same thing about their principals. At the turn of the century an economist named Wilfredo Pareto developed a principle of organizational behavior called the 80/20 rule. The idea was that generally 80% of the trouble that one encounters comes from 20% of the individuals in the organization. Think through this principle and you will find that it is true about 80% of the time. Whatever the case, the point is made that in any group setting you will generally have about 20% of the membership who may be questioning, argumentative or difficult to work with.

The Pareto Principle may be found to be accurate in many situations, but that doesn't mean it has to be considered as unchangeable. It is easy to blame difficulties and program faults upon the workers when, as Deming points out, the problem may be the system (1982). He suggests that no one should be blamed or penalized for performance that the individual is not able to govern. Usually, the problem student or teacher is not doing well, or creating difficulties for a reason, and the principal needs to discover the reason before making final decisions or lasting impressions.

MEETING INDIVIDUAL NEEDS

It is not humanly possible for the school leader to change the system, or even particular situations to meet the needs and desires of those who want something different. Imagine attempting to give one teacher his own classroom with a west exposure, another the specific students that she wants, another a preparation period after lunch, and another tables instead of desks. The list of expectations could be endless and making changes in certain ways does not mean that there is really any good reason for doing so.

Schooling is, in many respects, coming to terms with the multiple realities of people (Fullan, 1991). The principal who assumes automatically that everyone is on task, knows what is expected, and works in harmony to reach common desired ends, has not considered the expectations and realities of others, and is bound to end up with a headache and multiple frustrations. Individuals develop a particular style of behaving that they feel helps them to be successful around others. This behavior may persist even when others find it annoying or objectionable. School principals behave, too, by using speech and mannerisms that they have developed to help them get along with others. Some of these human communication patterns are very predictable and identifiable.

Thus, individuals with strong beliefs and convictions may be, as McCallister asserts, the observable ones with "noble" communication characteristics (1994). Individuals of this type are direct, straightforward, frank and spontaneous. They don't mind expressing their opinion or views at any time or place and often are seemingly intolerant of the thoughts of others. These individuals, if not worked with carefully, can create chaos in a faculty meeting or group setting, by disagreeing with suggestions, resisting the authority of the leader, and by directing others to a differing point of view.

Some individuals in a group may be consistently positive and are always displaying a happy, cheerful countenance. Cheerful people are usually concerned with establishing warm human relationships and do not like open conflict or hostile settings. At times, these individuals have difficulty making decisions, and they may be noncommittal on many issues.

McCallister suggests that leaders can achieve better results with their associates if they first, understand how they typically interact with others and second, what communication pattern others will predominantly use (pp. 22–46). She indicates that most individuals use one of three major communication patterns. These individuals are listed as the Noble, the Socratic, and the Reflective. The individual with a Noble pattern of communication, as previously noted, tends to use communication as a means to be blunt and say what he/she thinks. The Socratic individuals are verbose with an affinity for words. They like to discuss and analyze everything. Like the Greek philosopher Socrates, they prefer details and view argumentation and debate as desirable and constructive interactions. The Reflective person is concerned with human feelings above the content of interaction. This individual is a patient listener, and will often be flexible and persuadable. Reflectives will often ask in a meeting how a particular change or new policy will affect the morale, feelings and well-being of the participants. McCallister reports that blends of these three styles may create additional communication patterns that individuals use to interact with others (p. 31).

As difficult as it may be to be sensitive and understanding of others, school productivity and success require that the principal demonstrate consideration toward the feelings, attitudes, needs and intentions of co-workers. The emphasis is upon demonstrating rather than merely feeling consideration. The principal must "express" sensitivity in all types of interactions if building and maintaining positive relationships, and school morale are considered vital to success.

HANDLING REACTIVE CONFLICT SITUATIONS

Individuals respond differently to conflict and stress situations, and this knowledge can be of help to principals in understanding others and in reducing anxiety. I recall most vividly a situation in high school where I was serving as the school principal. We had been receiving three or four phone calls a week indicating that bombs were in the building ready to explode. Most often, these calls occurred at lunch time, and the callers had very youthful voices. Of course, the motive behind the calls was to empty the building of students and thereby delay class time while the school was being searched. Rather than play into the hands of the callers, the administrative staff decided that if a call came around the lunch hour and the voice was of high school age, we would investigate, but not announce the call to other faculty members, or empty the school of students and faculty.

During one of these calls, I had the custodians check the lockers in the area of school where a bomb was reported to be placed. As we were quietly searching the area, one of the teachers (normally a very quiet individual) came rushing out of her classroom wildly exclaiming, "Is there a bomb? Is my life in danger?" I attempted to explain the situation and what we were doing, but she was not pacified. "You're placing my life in danger by not emptying the building," she cried in a burst of anger and fear. At this point, she was almost uncontrollable and stated, "If a bomb goes off, I will hold you accountable." At this point, she marched back into the classroom. Needless to say, my anxiety rose about 100 points, and I was relieved that the bomb call was just another prank. I found that normally placid teachers can become very agitated if the right situation occurs that hits a sensitive issue or raises the fear of some threat either imaginary or real. The school principal must always be prepared to face this type of confrontation even when it is not expected. My solution was to invite the faculty to discuss issues of this nature and to receive their comments. Group discussion will generally help to relieve fears and provide the principal with the support that is needed.

Certainly, the teacher had a right to be concerned, and although the procedure had been discussed and approved in faculty meeting, the actual search of lockers in her area of the building was unsettling. The slight possibility of a bomb explosion created an increased fear in the individual for her safety and a resulting hostile feeling toward me. To better understand the nature of her reaction to this situation, and that of others as they approach conflict settings, it is helpful to understand how individuals respond to stress and conflict. Kenneth Thomas (1974) suggests that people approach conflict through one of five levels of involvement. These are: avoiding, accommodating, competing, compromising, or collaborating. These behaviors relate to how assertive individuals will become in being aggressive about meeting their own needs, rights and interests. Depending upon the situation, by creating conflict the individual may behave somewhere in a range from unassertive to assertive. In addition, individuals will often attempt to satisfy the concerns of others by being somewhere on a scale from uncooperative to cooperative.

The model, developed by Thomas (see Fig. 7.1) illustrates how individuals may be placed on a continuum as they react to conflict situations. As can be observed, individuals who tend to consider their own needs above those of others (assertive), and who are uncooperative, will react in a competitive manner during conflict. Individuals who are cooperative and basically unassertive, will be accommodating during conflict placing their needs second in order to satisfy concerns of others.

The dotted line in Figure 7.1 indicates a balance among competing and accommodating behaviors. An individual who avoids a conflict situation has a low assertive, and a low cooperative style. This might suggest that the individual is merely uninterested or withdrawn.

FIGURE 7.1

Handling Conflict of Roles and Responsibilities

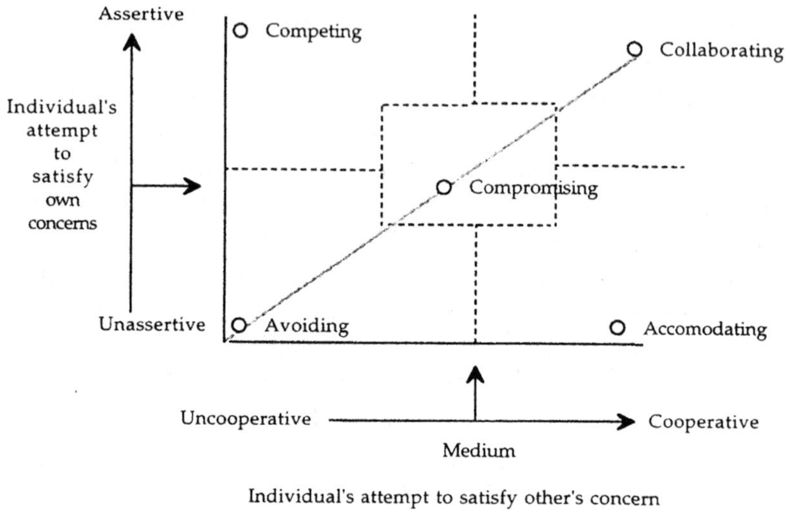

A compromising behavior suggests a medium assertive and a medium cooperative style. The individual at this level is somewhat concerned about satisfying his/her own concerns and not totally ready to meet the concerns of others, but is willing to compromise in order to best handle the conflict for all involved. This behavior reduces the conflict, but may not resolve the issue which could occur again without resolution.

Collaborative behavior is a result of high assertiveness and high cooperation. At this level, all parties are willing to work together to resolve problems and meet individual concerns. In a collaborative setting, the climate is one of trust, openness and mutual support necessary for the successful resolution of conflict, and problems that create adverse relationships.

At times, individuals who are frustrated will express that feeling even though the situation at hand has nothing to do with their frustrations. Insecurity, poor self-concept and some form of personal discouragement will create a climate for conflict. A school principal in one of my university graduate classes remarked that he had an experience with a hostile teacher in his school that really jolted his confidence. As a brand new principal at a junior high school (he was transferred from another school where he had been a vice principal), he was invited to sit in on a curriculum meeting with seven of the teachers from the school. The meeting was held during the summer so he had not yet made contact with any of the faculty members in the school. The committee was engaged in developing a curriculum design for the school and had been working on the project with the old principal for the entire preceding year. As introductions were being completed, one of the teachers, who had been closely observing the principal, remarked out loud, in dismay and disgust, "He's (the principal) even younger than I thought. How can they expect us to make changes in the school when they send a principal who is 'green as grass' and doesn't know anything? Doesn't the district office like our school? I am thinking of asking for a transfer."

The principal remarked to me that the other members of the committee seemed to be as shocked as he was. I asked him how he felt about the teacher's outburst and what he did at that point. "Well," he replied, "I felt like quitting right there. My heart was thumping, and I felt sick to my stomach. I didn't know if he was only speaking for himself or expressing the feelings of the committee, and maybe even the entire school faculty." He grinned and looked at me and said, "Why didn't you ever cover this type situation in your class on leadership?" I shrugged, felt somewhat sheepish and didn't respond. He continued, "After listening to his negative comments, I mustered some calmness and said, "I am sorry to hear you say those things about me. I'm sure that we both want the best for the students, and my age, or seeming lack of experience doesn't mean that I am any less interested or concerned than you are about what is best for the kids. I hope that you will continue to support this program as I do, and assist my efforts as principal to keep this a good school." This statement, the principal remarked, seemed to reduce the teacher's anxiety; and he was quiet the rest of the session. After the meeting, others on the committee came to the principal and expressed apologies for the teacher's conduct. They indicated that he was considered an outsider on the faculty and was often negative. "Were you relieved?" I asked. The principal said, "Yes, very much so, but I was concerned about my relationship with the teacher. Since then I have attempted to gain his friendship by going out of my way to talk to him, to ask for ideas, and to respond to his needs. He really is a lonely person. We seem to get along now, and he hasn't said a negative thing to me since the meeting."

Tact and avoiding anger are tools that principals can use to reduce the intensity of interactions and make it possible to build better relations in the future. Principals who keep calm in the face of disagreeable challenges will almost always gain respect from other staff members who may be present or hear reports about particular unsettling situations. Seeking compromises and helping others save face during disagreements can stretch the principal's patience, but the effort pays off because it diverts unnecessary confrontations so they can be handled in more appropriate settings and times (Muse, 1993).

BE PREPARED FOR THE UNEXPECTED

It is essential that school leaders be prepared to respond to questions, provide support when received, handle disputes, and give direction in any interactive setting in which they are involved. This doesn't mean that principals should always be in charge and chairing groups or committee meetings. What it does mean is that the principal must be prepared to react to unexpected information that comes forth—hostile feelings from members of a group toward others, and critical comments that might be directed toward you. Others expect the principal to be in charge in any school setting and handle confrontations before they get out of hand.

Obviously some caution should be taken not to take away the authority that you may have delegated to someone earlier to chair a meeting or lead some group activity. An example of this latter occurrence happened at a junior high school during one of the first school assemblies. The new assistant principal was delegated the responsibility for arranging and conducting the meeting by the principal. The assembly program involved a considerable amount of student business, which in the past had involved selecting student council members from the various classes. The principal, who was standing off stage in the auditorium, didn't like the noise level so he walked on stage, took the microphone from the vice principal, chastised the students for being too noisy and dismissed the student body to return to classes. The vice principal was upset because he hadn't been instructed before the assembly about what to expect from the students and how to conduct the meeting. He also felt that his leadership responsibility had been removed from him in front of the teachers and student body, and that the principal had made a serious error in judgment.

At times, unexpected situations may be very threatening and require immediate attention and action, as well as calmness and sound judgment from the school administrator. A few actual traumatic incidents that principals have had to face are:

- An uncontrollable, nude drug addict on the playground of an elementary school campus during recess period. The addict later collapsed and died on the sidewalk near the principal's office as a result of an overdose.
- A divorced parent who does not have child custody coming on campus and entering a classroom unannounced to take his/her child.
- Accidental death of a student on campus during school hours.
- Food poisoning of students from cafeteria food.
- Student walkout in protest over a school incident.
- Outbreak of fire and smoke in the building.
- Nearby industrial explosion causing damage to school as well as numerous student injuries.
- A plane crashes, killing members of a high school athletic team returning home from an event.
- Threat or actual occurrence of a tornado, blizzard, hurricane, or tsunami while school is in session.
- Bomb threat (a common incident that occurs at most junior and senior high schools).
- Gang fight on campus.

A school principal on the island of Kauai was faced with an unpleasant experience a few years ago when a deadly hurricane hit the island and caused major damages. The high school was a designated safety shelter, and although school was canceled in advance of the hurricane, the principal was expected to be on duty. His wife worked for the county government, and she was assigned at the county offices to assist in relief and maintenance efforts. This left two small school age children at home with an elderly grandmother. The phone lines went down early, and thus, for six hours, the principal did not know how his wife or his family at home were fairing. The school itself, which housed over 200 homeless residents, and a number of tourists, was slightly damaged, however, the principal's home was severely damaged. The grandmother and children escaped injury by hiding under the stair case. Importantly, the principal did not display his anxiety and stress about his family to those housed in his school. He remained calm and in control and carried out his responsibilities professionally.

In anticipation of serious incidents that may occur unexpectedly at school, many schools have established crisis teams. These teams, prepared to handle emergencies, swing into action if they are called to assist. Team responsibilities involve crowd control, counseling of involved individuals, establishing communication networks, scheduling information or inservice workshops, etc. In any crisis situation the principal must be prepared to assume responsive leadership, and by oral communication, maintain order, calmness and the confidence of those involved.

More common and less earthshaking than these incidents are the often frequent confrontations by upset, angry or tearful students, parents or teachers. These situations may often involve personality conflicts, and the principal must collect information about each case, and then give a considerable amount of time to the individuals who are involved. There are a few things that can be done by the principal to handle these situations.

- If possible, find a place in which you and the individuals can talk alone. Do not permit an issue (especially directed toward you by someone else) to become a stage production for others to hear.

- Remember that listening is always better than talking or telling.
- You don't always have to win an argument.
- Do not prematurely close off conversation unless the other person is becoming unreasonable and unmanageable.
- If you think that a particular session with an individual or group may be confrontational, do your homework. Collect all of the information that you can beforehand. Do not make statements that you are not sure of.
- In a confrontation session with an individual, attempt not to threaten. Use "I" messages as much as possible to reflect one's own thoughts and observations rather than imitate another's behavior. Beginning sentences with comments such as, "I am concerned. . . ," or, "I have noticed that. . . ,"are much less threatening than sentences that begin: "You have been late to school. . . ," or, "You are not pulling your. . . "
- To avoid confrontations at faculty meetings, always use a printed agenda. If a faculty member wants to initiate a debate or create a disruption, use the agenda as a reason to discuss that situation at a later time. Critics in a faculty will often attempt to use meetings in which the total staff is present in order to present their complaints and to attempt to gain group support.

DIFFICULT PERSONALITY TYPES

The following are some of the personality types that are not easy to work with. The suggestions offered for each of the personalities will assist you in handling these people and working through the problems that they present.

RELUCTANT INDIVIDUALS

In every classroom and among a group of teachers there will be a few individuals who seldom speak or contribute to discussions. The reasons for this type of conduct may vary from an apparent lack of interest in the goals of a committee or meeting, a feeling of discomfort in speaking, an unwillingness to compete with overbearing or dominant group members or a quiet personality. Such behavior does not mean that the individual is not knowledgeable, or isn't capable of adequate expression in other areas.

The issue is usually one of getting the quiet teachers to add to the productivity of a committee or group meeting. The principal will need to use group activities that encourage the reluctant teachers to participate. The principal can involve group members by:

- Assigning the quiet teachers topics or ideas to report on in which they are involved or have experience.
- Informing the committee or group that you want feedback on a program, project or issue by having everyone comment.
- Breaking up committees or groups into smaller numbers to work on specific parts of an assignment. The fewer the numbers the more apt the quiet teachers will become involved in the discussions.
- Ask the quiet teacher later in a one-on-one setting how things are going in the meeting(s) and if the teacher has any specific suggestions to make.

OVERBEARING INDIVIDUALS

These individuals seem to think that they know all of the answers, and that their expertise is of utmost importance. If permitted, they will wield a disproportionate amount of influence in a group. Overbearing group members use statements such as:

- "What you don't understand is . . . "
- "You're not listening to what I am . . . "
- "I'm ready to move on to another . . . "
- "We tried that before and it didn't work."
- "My advice is to do this . . . "
- "It seems that we all agree to . . . "

Overbearing or pushy individuals are often trying to get attention and to show others that they have a lot of ability. Often, however, their very desire to be important causes behaviors that are unwelcome by other members of the group.

The principal can best handle these individuals by recognizing their contributions, but also by making it possible for others to contribute. If it is possible, contact these individuals in advance of a meeting and ask for their support in helping others to contribute. It may also be feasible to assign overbearing members responsibilities that use their talents, but limit their opportunities to make excessive comments and proposals about every topic that is discussed. Finally, agree at the onset of meetings that all group members need to have an opportunity to present their views. Limit discussion to a set time period and monitor the times that an individual may speak.

DOMINATING INDIVIDUALS

The principal needs to be cautious if one of these individuals is a vice principal, counselor, or other individual with a leadership responsibility. If this is the case, then a change of communication style is necessary in order to give faculty an opportunity to contribute. Dominating personality types will consume whatever time that they can in a meeting. They always have a hand up and may even interrupt if the opportunity presents itself. Dominators are not necessarily aggressive or overbearing, but just like to talk and think about possibilities until everyone is ready to close the meeting and go home. The constant talk of these individuals can create boredom and frustration at faculty meetings, lack of committee productivity, and long sessions with the principal in one-on-one interactions. The principal can best handle these individuals in a polite but firm manner. Comments such as, "We need to hear from everyone," or "______________ (person's name) would you hold some of your comments for later so we can keep on schedule," will help to bridle the constant talking pattern of these individuals. At times, prior to a meeting, have a short discussion with a dominator about sharing the speaking time.

CRITICAL AND COMPLAINING INDIVIDUALS

These individuals tend to be negative about the way school is going and are very verbal in pointing out school weaknesses. Critics and complainers have a need to tell others what is bothering them and hope to gather support for their concerns. Typical comments coming from those who criticize are:

- "He always uses favorites and doesn't give others a chance."
- "Why are we pushing this plan? It was tried 20 years ago and didn't work."
- "This principal isn't as good as the one we had before."
- "Students are creating more problems in school this year, and it is because the principal isn't tough enough."
- "The principal doesn't need to have faculty meetings last so long."
- "I knew the principal's new hall pass plan wouldn't work. He didn't listen to the right teachers."

Individuals who complain, or "cry wolf" all of the time about the way things are going may lose their credibility with others and be ignored. But the frequent harping about issues that have emotional impact with the other teachers may gain adherents, and create confusion and bad feelings. Principals should not ignore the critics. They may, at times, be truly reflecting the feelings of others. Their comments may point out important obstacles to a plan or program that has been overlooked.

In dealing with critical or negative comments, Belasco (1990) recommends direct face-to-face interaction with the critic. This action will let the individual know that the comments he or she is making are not accepted by others, that the negative comments interfere with the progress of the group, or that you would prefer that the individual discuss these items with you in private. If the comments are inaccurate, the principal will have an opportunity to question the individual's motives and also give correct information. The principal should point out that rumors hurt others, are not good for morale and that if the individual is concerned about the value of a program or policy, that person should come to the source for correct information.

A number of other strategies can be used to defuse the activities of critics. The principal can:

- Attempt to short circuit the network that critics use to tell others about concerns. Visit key individuals in the school and ask them how things are going. They will often be able to tell you if a faculty member is upset about any program or policy.
- Use faculty meetings and committee get-togethers to present information about topics that critics are concerned about.
- Keep in touch with the school's critics and complainers. Ask for their advice and listen to their concerns. Often you will receive valuable information and ideas about how to make improvements in a problem area.
- Enlist the aid and support of the critic by asking the individual to be responsible for a part of the activity in question. It is easier to criticize from outside a program than it is when you are a part of it.
- Collect as much information as you can about the issues, programs or policies that are upsetting to the complainers. Be sure that you are able to explain why something is being done a certain way. When possible, evaluate the process to see if results are positive.

At times, all of us become critics when a particular idea presented by others doesn't seem be the best thing to do. Criticism provides an opportunity to view an issue from more than one point of view. Complaining, however, often leads to resentment and feelings of dissatisfaction toward the individuals involved, because the complaints are often said to others rather than the people responsible. The principal should keep an open mind, and an open office door for those who feel uneasy or unhappy about a decision that might be made. When the critic does express a point of view contrary to yours, express appreciation for the individual's comments and provide as much information as you can supporting the task, program or policy under question. If appropriate, ask the critic for advice on how best to make the activity work, and ask for assistance. Finally, check back with the critic occasionally to see if feelings have improved, and if the individual can give any additional valuable feedback that will help the program in question succeed.

SUMMARY

Maintaining positive relationships with individual staff members, students, parents, and others is a difficult challenge. Managing conflict and the actions of difficult individuals is a larger part of a principal's job. Individuals may create conflict as a result of breaking school policy, questioning school goals, disagreeing with administrator decision making, and varying value orientations. Often the value orientations create the most difficulty, as some individuals seem to be totally out of harmony with the administrator's vision and goals for the school. If possible, a win-win approach to working with difficult individuals is the most desirable solution. This action requires that the principal find solutions to working together that satisfies both parties. Often the principal must be assertive, and initiate frequent discussions with the individual, or individuals who are creating conflict. This process helps to determine the nature of the problems, the attitudes of the parties involved and procedures that must be taken to resolve the issue—at least to that point.

FACULTY MEETINGS

Faculty meetings are essential "get-togethers" for the principal and staff to conduct business, resolve problems, share ideas and to build group solidarity. Principals know what to do at faculty meetings, but often add these elements to make the meetings an unpleasant experience.

- Waste time.
- Criticize school performance.
- Ramble, and add items for discussion not on agenda.

- Go overtime.
- Let certain individuals who like to talk monopolize the meetings.
- Discuss items that only refer to one or two faculty members.

Rather than do the above the principal should:

- Begin faculty meeting on time (regardless of attendance) and end on time.
- Recognize the performance of faculty members who have accomplished some tasks, or have distinguished themselves since the previous meeting.
- Prepare an agenda and follow it.
- Be sensitive to group dynamics. Encourage teacher comments, but do not permit individuals to dominate discussion with personal agendas.

BIBLIOGRAPHY

Belasco, J.A. (1990). *Teaching the Elephant to Dance: The Managers Guide to Empowering Change*. New York: Crown Publishers Inc., p. 41.

Deming, W.E. (1986) *Out of the Crisis*. Cambridge, MA: Massachusetts Institute of Technology., pp. 250–51.

Fullam, M.G. (1991). *The New Meaning of Educational Change*. New York: Teachers College Press., p. 95.

McCallister, L. (1994). *I Wish I'd Said That*! New York: John Wiley and Sons, Inc., p. 64.

Muse, I., & others. (1993). "Sensitivity." *Principals for our Changing Schools*. S. Thompson, ed. Fairfax, VA: National Policy Board for Educational Administration, pp. 15–18.

Purkey, W.W. (1984). *Inviting School Success*. Belmont, CA: Wadsworth Publishing Co., p. 2.

Thomas, K. (1976). "Conflict and Conflict Management." *Handbook of Industrial and Ogranizational Psychology*. M. Dunnette, ed. Chicago: Rand McNally.

8

The Principal as a Speech Giver

An honest tale speeds best being plainly told. —*William Shakespeare*

Like it or not, principals are expected to give speeches on occasions. School administrators often feel relaxed when talking to students or teachers as a group, but when asked to speak outside of the school setting, feel ill at ease and apprehensive. A few principals adopt the attitude of just saying, "No, I am too busy." They are fearful of making a mistake, do not feel that they present well or that they have nothing to say that would be of any importance.

One of the difficulties with the "reluctant principal" as a speech giver, is the missed opportunities to market and sell the school. If schools are to be effective and maintain or generate community understanding and support, the principal needs to be involved in a variety of civic activities. The National Association of Elementary School Principals (1991, p. 7) stresses that principals need to capitalize on opportunities to speak in order to highlight student achievement, underscore the school's mission, and honestly and openly address questions and problems.

Whether it is to inform, persuade, give support or praise the efforts of others, the principal must exercise the leadership responsibility of public speaking. Giving a speech to a particular group doesn't have to be a chilling adventure, or a lesson in humility. Public speaking is, to a large degree, a skill, and with practice, and a few good "do's and don'ts," you can have a very presentable performance on any occasion. One point to remember is that enthusiasm and preparation will usually carry a speaker to the end of a successful performance. It is not necessary to be a natural orator and polished speaker to do well at the speaker's stand.

There are a number of important ideas to think about when accepting and preparing for the delivery of a speech. These ideas or steps are:

- Prepare yourself for success.
- Consider the purpose and audience.
- Prepare what you know well.
- Deliver your best shot and keep it brief.

Use these steps as guides while preparing your speech, and you will find the task much easier and more rewarding.

PREPARE YOURSELF FOR SUCCESS

When you are asked to give a speech, consider the request an honor, and accept graciously. There are few others in your school setting who have the total picture of the school, its mission and your aspirations for school improvement. McElroy and Schrader (1986) speak of occasions when a member within an organization must assume a star role in the communication process. The principal often assumes this central role because he or she has the greatest access to the information about the school, its programs, and achievements.

Remember that as the speaker you have the advantage of knowing your topic and in being able to present the ideas that you are most interested in. Typically, you have been asked to speak because some group will be interested in knowing more about your ideas on education, the happenings at your school, the achievements of your students or the results of some program that is underway. Few listeners want to attend a speech to hear the speaker fail. They want you to succeed, and they want to learn more about the subject that you will present. The more confident you are and the more enthusiasm that you display, the more likely the audience will feel that you have shared something worthwhile with them.

CONSIDER THE PURPOSE AND AUDIENCE

A school principal can be asked to speak at almost any occasion, ranging in scope and audience from that of a Boy Scout honors night program to a civic group banquet. Principals have been asked to speak at functions ranging from funerals and retirement dinners to sports awards banquets, PTA meetings, church functions, and school graduations.

While you will most often be asked to speak on some topic of education, about which you are very knowledgeable, there will always be an occasion when common sense will suggest that you decline as the speaker. When it is obvious that the purpose of the speech involves a political conflict, hidden agenda or power struggle, it is usually best to not participate.

When told the purpose of the meeting and the desire of the group for you to participate, make sure that you are very clear as to the subject that will be presented. If possible, ask the requester what leeway you have in approaching the subject. It is always a big help to the speaker to be able to choose a topic that is of interest, and one you know a lot about. As a help in guiding your topic presentation, ask yourself these relevant questions:

- What is the age, interest and background of the audience?
- How important is the subject to the audience?
- Will the audience have particular views and opinions about the subject?
- Do I know the audience, and how well do they consider my credibility as a speaker and as a school leader?

The first step in answering these questions might be to review with the program chairperson each of the audience items with which you have a concern. If you know members of the expected audience, you could also give them a call and discuss your interest in meeting their interests and expectations.

Often, the group requesting your participation, and the purpose of the event, will describe the audience. For instance, if you are speaking at an awards banquet, the audience will be composed of parents and relatives eager to hear about the accomplishments of their children. Your remarks should be addressed to that group, and focus upon the values of hard work, family support, teacher encouragement and student effort. Talking to a civic or business organization will involve adults who are educated and highly interested in the education of youth. Your task with this group is to inform them of school happenings and to inspire them with your mission of schooling and what it can become. Schools are interesting places, and you should have many stories that are engaging, humorous and uplifting.

ADJUSTING TO THE SITUATION

Flexibility is a must when speaking to large groups, as anything can go wrong before or during a presentation. A number of years ago the very popular and well known historian, Max Lerner, was speaking to a large community group in a school auditorium in Denver, Colorado. The building was packed and everything technical had been tested a number of times to ensure a trouble free evening. But as might be expected, the sound system went dead three minutes into the speaker's presentation. Without losing his poise, stage presence or the attention of the audience, Lerner, with his rich, deep voice, stepped to the side of the podium and remarked with a smile, "It has been said that I speak so loudly that I don't need a microphone, so with your support, I will continue." The audience adjusted by listening carefully, the speaker spoke clearly and with authority, and the evening was considered a definite success. On the other hand, a student giving a presentation at a Future Farmers Conference was not prepared to handle an embarrassing incident during his speech. As he was speaking, the young man slapped the podium with both hands to make a point. The force of his hands striking the podium caused it to tip and fall from the stage to the floor of the auditorium. With considerable embarrassment, the speaker collected his notes while others returned the podium to the stage. The young man was so distraught that he lost his composure and struggled through the balance of his presentation.

Be positive and flexible as you approach the speaker's stand. If circumstances create an awkward speaking situation (such as speaking while dessert is being served, the pre-speaker announcements taking too long, or only three people showing up for the meeting and presentation, etc.), adjust, and regulate your talk to the situation. The organizers of the meeting, and the people attending will understand and appreciate your willingness to carry on.

PREPARING THE SPEECH

A good speech is one that is presented enthusiastically, draws attention to ideas and not the speaker, is well-organized and finishes on time.

Enthusiastic speakers avoid pitfalls that distract from the presentation. To be most effective, a speaker will:

- Develop an interesting introduction, body and conclusion to the speech.
- Practice the talk until he or she can speak in a relaxed manner and use body language effectively.
- Use facts, examples and stories in the speech that add interest and audience involvement.
- Use clear and colorful language.
- Read from your written material as little as possible. Listeners want you to be natural and to establish eye contact.
- Preparation should give special attention to the major segments of the speech: the introduction, the body and the conclusion.

THE INTRODUCTION

The introduction of a speech must gain the immediate attention of the audience. The first words that come out of the speaker's mouth can interest the listeners or close minds. Remember that it is words that are important, not questionable attention getters. Slamming a book on the podium in order to make a loud noise, or dropping 40 sheets of paper as you approach the speaker's stand, and exclaiming, "Oh, there goes my talk," may draw attention, but can also be trite, or unappealing to the audience.

The introduction should be brief and interesting. The purpose of the introduction is to lead the audience directly to the body of your message. There are three deadly "do nots" when giving an introduction:

- *Prefacing Remarks* Do not preface remarks with excuses or problems that you have had in preparing for the speech. Comments like those that follow can turn off an audience quickly:
    - "I didn't ask to speak to you, but . . . "
    - "I was just asked yesterday to speak so I am not as prepared . . . "
    - "If any of you want to leave before I begin my talk, now is a good time."
    - "I want to tell you about the traffic ticket I received on the way. . . . "

  The audience did not come to hear you give negative self talk. These types of comments distract from the presentation and make it difficult for you to communicate positively to the audience.
- *Apologizing* Do not let the audience know how bad you will be as a presenter before you even begin. Most poor talks result from inadequate preparation, not from lack of communication skills. Speakers that comment, "I am not a good public speaker so bear with me," or "Someone else should be giving this speech," will certainly help to convince the audience that you are, indeed, the wrong person to be speaking.
- *Distracting Clichés or Offensive Language* Clichés are words or phrases that may have, at one time, seemed catchy and interesting, but with overuse have become stale and unoriginal. When a speaker states, "I'm sure that you have all heard the story. . . ," the immediate response is why would the audience want to hear it again.

> Some stories even with good moral value, have been heard so many times that to hear them again elicits a groan from the audience. The groan, although politely suppressed, is even greater when the speaker, thinking the worn out cliché to be original, pauses and waits for the audience to laugh. Some clichés are often too trite or "corny," to be used as an attention getter. Comments such as, "Good horse sense in a school situation is stable thinking," or "I would like to be a pessimist, but it wouldn't work out," may be amusing with some audiences, but not all. If you are concerned about the overuse of a story or cliché, try it out with a friend or two and get their advice. If they have heard it, it is best to not use it in your talk.
>
> Movies are often filled with crude and risque language, or slang designed primarily to get a laugh and to sell the film as an adult movie for mature audiences. The auditorium and banquet hall are not theaters, and audiences listening to a speaker are offended by off-color jokes and crude stories. Keep your comments clean and uplifting. Poor taste doesn't sell speeches in the school business.

Humor is one technique used to capture the interest and attention of the listeners. A clever and appropriate story or item of wit is useful and works if you personally feel comfortable with that approach. Many interesting anecdotes or quotes can be turned to fit almost any occasion. For instance, if you are talking about teamwork or leadership, everyone can sympathize with how difficult it is to get 100% cooperation. Casey Stengel, a baseball manager, had a good analogy of leadership when he quipped, "Keep the five guys on the team who hate your guts, away from the four who are still undecided."

Another humorous technique is to poke good-natured fun at a well-liked person in the audience, or one of the group's leaders. At a meeting with all the teachers in a school district, the speaker used this story about one of the popular English teachers:

"Mrs. Bell is, as I understand, a very good teacher in English at the high school. In one of her classes she was reviewing the students knowledge of the names of the states. She said to one of her students, 'Charlie, I'm disappointed that you can't recite all of the states by memory. Why, when I was your age, I could do them all.' 'Yes, Mrs. Bell,' the young man replied, 'But when you were my age, there were only 13 states to remember.'"

Simple one line statements can also be amusing if the audience is prepared and knows that you are intending to be humorous. Some examples of one-liners are:

- "The only thing a teenager will take lying down these days is a telephone call."
- A kindergartner in frustration said, 'They make you start school when you can't read or write and then tell you not to talk.'"
- "My teacher does a bird imitation, she watches me like a hawk."
- "A really ill student is one who gets sick on Saturday."
- "Don't expect much of a school when half of the students are below average."
- "Insanity is finding something that doesn't work and doing more of it."

If you do use humor in a speech, be cautious that the topic or individuals referred to in the story line will not be offensive to members of the audience. References to lack of mental ability, a person's weight, age or attractiveness, race, physical disability or gender, may not be found amusing by some individuals in the audience. Timm (1993) recommends that the speaker use wit and not jokes. He suggests that almost any presentation can be improved by a little humor. Being witty involves the use of a humorous remark, story, incident at school, cartoon, etc., that makes you chuckle and might do the same for the audience. Don't attempt to be funny just for the purpose of making the audience laugh unless you have a proven track record of tying wit to educational happenings. When in doubt about using a joke, or an amusing story, the best policy is to leave it at home. You do not want to run the risk of looking foolish or offending others when it is not necessary.

Humor should orient the audience in some way to the topic or idea that you will be addressing. Osborn and Osborn (1991) suggests that humor in a speech creates identification by building relationships, relieving tension, and reminding the listener that there is a human element in all situations, and that we should not take ourselves too seriously. Humor also helps convince an audience that you are active, articulate and interested in your subject. Lighter experiences can often be found in amusing incidents that happen on a daily basis. A team member missing a bus to a game, a teacher locked out of a classroom or a principal going to the wrong city to attend a meeting can easily be turned into a humorous story. Animation when speaking will also help hold the attention of an audience. This is especially true if the speaker wishes to exaggerate or overemphasize comical situations to a funny situation. Humor at any time can be deadly if it is perceived as offensive or in some way alienates the audience. The use of a funny anecdote that is in good taste will help hold audience attention, especially if the audience is restless or the topic is overly technical or factual.

THE BODY OF THE TALK

Most speeches that principals give are designed to inform the listeners about some aspect of the school program. On occasion, a speech may be to persuade the audience to support some event or program, such as a fund-raising drive, a board issue, a kindergarten reading program, cooperative learning and so forth. In any event, the principal wants the audience to understand exactly what the purpose of the presentation will be and what he or she would like the listeners to do or think as a result of the speech. DeVito (1988) refers to this latter part as promoting audience need. A need must exist for the program that is in operation or is being proposed. For example, recently a school district became concerned about drugs in the schools and wanted to place into policy and practice a firm new set of school regulations regarding disciplinary actions to be taken if students brought, sold, or used drugs on campus.

The high school principal, in particular, spoke at a number of community gatherings about the proposed policy. At these meetings, drug use by youth in the nation and state was emphasized as well as the current situation in the community. It was pointed out that drug use on campus affects those at home, as well as in the schools. For the new policy to be effective, it was stressed that the community needed to be supportive.

When the goal of the principal is to persuade the audience that a need or problem exists, a plan should be recommended to answer, resolve, or satisfy the need. If support is expected of the audience, it should be emphasized, and specifically stated before the speech is concluded. An action may involve the audience's support by voting, volunteering or participating.

The best speeches are focused, to the point, and contain no more than three or four main points. Other ideas to keep in mind that will help create a good speech are:

- Keep the flow of your speech logical and interesting.
- Use facts, examples, and stories to highlight and illustrate your speech.
- Use personal examples to make the presentation warm and inviting.
- Don't overuse educational jargon. Terms such as "interface," "pedagogical factors," "systems thinking," "strategic ambiguity," and "technological determinism," may boost the speaker's feeling of knowledge and authority but will leave the audience unimpressed.
- Keep your talk current by being well read and up-to-date on what is happening in your field on a local, state and national level. You never know when you will be asked a question about a current issue in education and it is important to be well read. You may also discover in your reading, an important item of interest that can be used in this or another speech.

CONCLUSION

The conclusion of a speech should always come at the right time—that is, when you have completed what it is you want to say, and when the audience has had enough to feel satisfied. Speeches should usually never go more than 20 to 30 minutes unless there is a question and answer period following the presentation. The conclusion exists to give the speech a crisp and definite end. At the conclusion of your talk do not be in the position that you have to say, "I'm sorry that I went overtime," "Oh, where did the time go, I was just getting started," or "Let me take just another minute." A good conclusion summarizes the key points of the speech and ends with a thought, quote, or positive statement. If appropriate, you may want to thank the audience for inviting you and for their attention.

LOOK SHARP, FEEL SHARP, BE SHARP

Your delivery is the most visual and selling part of what you say. Most audiences are pleased that the school principal is going to be the speaker. They respect this position, and when you speak they will listen intently and observe you carefully. Everything that you do from the time that you sit on the stage, until you begin your talk is also part of your performance. It goes without saying that dress is important. If you are in doubt as what to wear, ask the host or others who have attended a similar event. When the decision is left up to you, it is usually a good rule to dress up rather than down. I prefer knowing that if I am dressed too formally, I can remove my coat and even a tie, if necessary, to look more casual.

Do not appear nervous when sitting on the stage. Smile and look happy to be in attendance. This is the time to begin to make eye contact. Your personality and frame of mind will begin to show long before you say your first words. No matter how much you want to review your notes one last time, sitting on the stage is not the place to practice or engage in a rewrite. Another behavior that often looks awkward is when the speaker makes last second adjustments to clothing, hair, or makeup. The time to recheck grooming is before you walk on the stage, not as you approach the podium.

After you have been introduced, and as you approach the speaker's stand, pay attention to posture and your behavior. Do not carry a number of books to the stand, and certainly do not bring a briefcase. The audience will focus more attention on those objects than they will on what you are going to say. Do not wait until you reach the podium before you take your notes from a pocket or reach for your reading glasses. Many speakers do this, and it is irritating to the audience to sit while someone is getting ready to talk. Another caution is to not blow your nose, clear your throat or take a drink of water in preparation for your initial comments. The first two actions can be considered ill-mannered, and the drinking of water might make members of the audience think more about how thirsty they are than about what you are going to say.

A few school principals have interacted with groups so much that a speech is just another occasion to them. These individuals appear perfectly relaxed when they speak, and they immediately connect with the audience in a personal way. However, it is possible to be too relaxed and informal. Speakers should not lean on the podium and should be cautious to keep their elbows at their sides and not on the podium. Attention to these details will be to your advantage as you prepare to speak.

Effective presentations to groups come with practice and preparation. Small details, if handled well, can enhance you as a speaker and create a good speech. To be an effective speaker and improve your chances of doing a good job, follow these hints:

- Sound natural and be enthusiastic.
- Avoid distracting mannerisms.
- Smile and speak up (practicing in front of a mirror at home will help).
- Have something interesting to say.
- Practice your speech.
- Use eye contact with your audience.
- Use body language to add physical emphasis and feeling to your presentation.

- Be respectful to your host and audience.
- Always be positive.

On occasion, you will be asked to present some information to a group that is more of an inservice training presentation than a formal speech. During these events, the presenter needs to be less formal and more relaxed with the audience. In these situations, such as speaking to a group of principals, teachers or university faculty, a little advance planning can pay big dividends during and after the presentation. I typically ask for a list of those who plan on being present, and if they have a title, or perform some school function, I include that with their names. I also ask the individual in charge of the event to point out to me individuals who are well liked, noted for some recent award or who like to laugh and enjoy themselves at conferences. By arriving early, it is possible to meet a few of these individuals and remember names, and faces. Then, in my presentation, I try to call those people by first name when the situation calls for an interaction to take place. For example, you might drop names when you reach a point where you want some participation or increased audience attention:

- "Tom, will you and Mary come up? I want to illustrate a point."
- "Sally, you teach English. What is your biggest frustration with giving homework assignments?"
- "Where is Andy? Andy, I heard that you discovered a new way to sleep in the faculty room, and as a result, missed your fourth period class on Tuesday. What is your secret?"
- "I understand that Ms. Lee was voted teacher of the year last week. I took up a collection from the faculty and threw in a dollar myself, so I am pleased to ask Ms. Lee to come up and accept this crisp new $1.00 bill for a job well done."

Comments such as these are fun and help the group to relax. In particular, the ones called by name are very pleased, as well as surprised that they are getting some attention.

When speaking to a small group, or when it is appropriate to be more friendly and informal with an audience, abandoning the podium and microphone might improve the presentation. Often when there are only a few listeners, the podium and microphone puts too much distance between the speaker and listeners. Some speakers in an effort to relate more to their audiences will remove the microphone from its stand then walk in front of the podium to deliver their speech. This friendly approach adds life to a presentation, gives the audience something to look at that is nearby and helps to personalize a message. Of course, you must be comfortable with this approach, and, in particular, you must be capable of presenting your ideas without reading from a prepared text.

SUMMARY

How you present yourself when giving a speech will make a lasting impression about yourself and the job that you hold. The speaker's influence will be enhanced by being considerate of the audience. Everyone relates to a likable person who makes them feel comfortable. To get off to a good start in a speech, smile, be enthusiastic and talk so your listeners can understand what you are trying to say. Lastly, be sensitive to your audience. Prepare in advance so that those listening will know that you have made a sincere effort to meet their interests and needs.

APPEARANCE

You never get a second chance to make a first impression. Dress and grooming most often determine what a first impression will be, and what you say will come second. Check your school appearances by answering these specific questions:

- Do I check my clothes each morning and evening to see if they are clean, pressed and appropriate for the occasion?

- Do I ask advice from others on what clothes look the best on me considering weight, height, hair color and complexion?
- Am I free of bad breath? If you are not sure, keep a bottle of mouth wash in your desk at school and use it frequently. It is not a bad idea to keep a toothbrush and paste at school for noon time usage.
- Do I keep my hair trimmed and groomed?
- Do I exercise frequently so I feel good and have good muscle tone?

BIBLIOGRAPHY

DeVito, J. (1988). *Human Communication: The Basic Course.* 4th ed. New York: Harper & Row, Publishers, Inc., p. 333.

McElroy, J., & Schrader, C., (1986) "Attribution Theories of Leadership and Network Analysis." *Journal of Management 12*, pp. 351–362.

National Association of Elementary School Principals. (1991). *Proficiencies for Principals.* 1615 Duke Street, p. 7.

Osborn, M. & Osborn, S. (1991). *Public Speaking.* 2nd ed. Boston: Houghton Mifflin Co., p. 404.

Timm, P. (1993). *Basics of Oral Communication.* Cincinnati: South-Western Publishing Co., p. 123.

9781883001278